PUB

West Yorkshire

FORTY CIRCULAR WALKS
AROUND WEST YORKSHIRE INNS

Leonard Markham

COUNTRYSIDE BOOKS
NEWBURY, BERKSHIRE

COUNTRYSIDE BOOKS
3 Catherine Road
Newbury, Berkshire

ISBN 1 85306 222 7

Photographs by the author
Maps by Ian Streets
Cover illustration by Colin Doggett

Produced through MRM Associates Ltd., Reading
Typeset by Paragon Typesetters, Queensferry, Clwyd
Printed in England by J. W. Arrowsmith Ltd., Bristol

Contents

Introduction

Powerhouse of the north, West Yorkshire is rarely associated with the great outdoors, adventurous 'soles' generally gravitating to the dales and moors for their weekend hikes. But walkers need not stray. Within this surprising county a variety of routes beckon – proud city trails, oasis walks between the conurbations, quiet village strolls and moorland tramps – some spiked with the history and archaeology of our industrial past, and all within easy reach of the most welcoming of inns.

The sketch map which accompanies each walk is designed to give a simple yet accurate idea of the route to be taken. For those who like a more detailed map, the relevant number in the OS Landranger 1:50 000 series is also given. Please remember the Country Code and make sure gates are not left open or any farm animals disturbed.

No special equipment is needed to enjoy the countryside on foot, but do wear a stout pair of shoes and remember that at least one muddy patch is likely even on the sunniest day. Do please also remember that even the most accommodating of inn landlords is unlikely to welcome walkers with muddy boots, so leave yours outside the pub when you return.

Many of the walks in this book recommend leaving your car in the inn car park, with the intention of eating or drinking at the inn on your return. If you do so, particularly outside normal opening hours, please ask the landlord's permission. A car left for hours in an otherwise empty car park may become an object of suspicion.

There are 40 good walks and 40 good pubs within these pages. I have chosen mostly short, easy gradient routes so that even those of average fitness need have no fear of fatigue. This, my second volume in an already popular series of pub walk books, offers tried and tested recipes for blissful days, combining the delights of the open track and the hand-pulled, home-cooked pleasures of the bar.

Leonard Markham
Barwick-in-Elmet

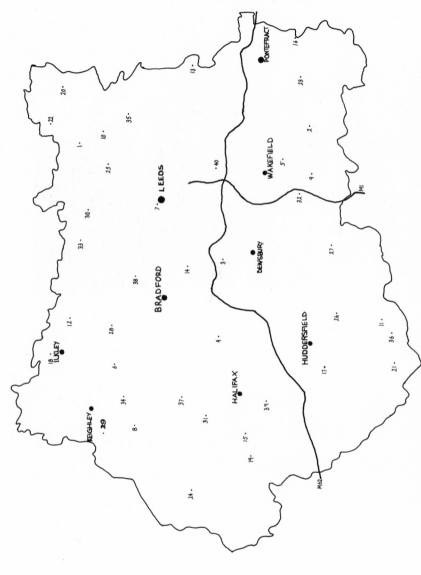

Area map of West Yorkshire showing location of the walks.

Bardsey
The Bingley Arms

Billed as England's oldest inn, the Bingley Arms has drained a sea of ale since travelling monks quaffed their first pints in AD 953. Bearing the accretions and alterations of a hundred reigns, boasting beams, figured stones, mysterious priest holes and a secret passageway, the inn rejoices in its history, offering a menu echoing the pageant of England past.

Two period bars lit by yawning fireplaces and hung with ancient deeds and indentures, serve a changing variety of bar meals. The Yorkshire rarebite (an award winning Yorkshire pudding) heads the retinue of starters which also include home-made soups and patés. Main courses always feature a savoury pie of the day, together with lamb cutlets, chicken kiev, lasagne, a range of omelettes and hot sandwiches. Vegetarians are well provided for by the Bingley Arms stir fry, the courgette wheel (a choux pastry ring filled with pan fried courgettes, tomatoes, herbs and cheese) and the vegetable moussaka. Children are welcome for meals and summer barbecues are held on the terraced beer garden to the rear. Men of the cloth still swear by the inn's excellent brews – creamy Tetley Mild and Bitter, Marston's

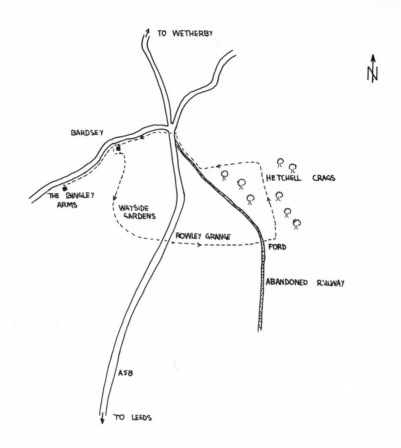

Pedigree, Carlsberg, Castlemaine and Lowenbrau lagers, Gaymer's Olde English cider and draught Guinness being finely presented alongside a generous selection of celebratory wines.

Diners who wish to toast the occasion could well go the whole hog, finding wild boar on the menu of the trophied banqueting chambers upstairs. This restaurant, open every evening, offers game aplenty. Come in period dress and feast on pheasant, wild duck, sautéd wood pigeon, venison or jugged hare. Or would you prefer the Henry V Agincourt steak, the salmon Wellington, lamb Brontë, red snapper or sovereigns of pork?

The Bingley Arms is open Monday to Friday from 12 noon to 3 pm and 5.30 pm to 11 pm. Saturday and Sunday hours are from 12 noon to 11 pm.

Telephone: 01937 572462.

How to get there: The inn is off the A58 Leeds to Wetherby road, in the village of Bardsey.

Parking: Park in the inn car park.

Length of the walk: 2 miles. OS Map Landranger series 104 (inn GR 364431).

An easy family amble through a nature reserve: ideal for youngsters. There is a chance to search for a rare type of millipede in the reserve. It's hard to keep clean while pursuing these thousand legged monsters − so dig out the wellies and the old clothes!

The Walk

Turn right from the inn and walk round the bend to the lych gate of All Hallows. Turn right through the green wicket gate along a signposted footpath. Turn left along the bottom of the churchyard and turn right opposite the back porch on a descending path. Cross a stream and continue uphill to a field, veering diagonally right across the corner to the field edge near housing. Still climbing, proceed forward and merge with an access track at the crest. Walk on, passing Wayside Gardens to your left. Cross the busy A58 and take a marked footpath 20 yards to your left, turning right past the derelict Rowley Grange. Ignore the next footpath to your right and keep on towards the line of an abandoned railway. Drop down under an old bridge, and using the ford, enter Hetchell Wood (a Yorkshire Wildlife Trust nature reserve). Out with the magnifying glasses! The aforementioned monsters, known only from a dozen or so sites in Britain, inhabit the crags above. Rare little millipedes, *geoglomeris jurassica*, they share their splendid dell with yellow archangel, toothwort, redstarts, siskins and owls.

Turn left, follow the streamside path and emerge from the reserve, continuing streamside uphill to meet a path from the right. Turn left. After 200 yards, bear right through woodland and cross a stile, taking the footpath on your right hand. Walk on, above and parallel to the A58, and drop down to the road opposite Church Lane. Take Church Lane back into Bardsey.

Other local attractions: The Anglo Saxon church of All Hallows and the nearby market town of Wetherby (horse racing).

Wintersett
The Anglers Retreat

The isolated Anglers Retreat, once blighted by nearby opencast coal mining, has recently blossomed alongside an impressive restoration scheme. A rarely flowering bloom seldom open midweek except on sunny summer days and bank holidays, the inn is well worth seeking out at weekends. Nicknamed 'The Sett', this proud and distinctively independent free house has a small plush lounge and a cosy part flagged bar displaying photographs of the locally moribund mining industry. Proudly burnished miner's lamps, a treasury of tally discs and an open coal fire keep the memories bright.

The inn serves hand-pulled Tetley and Theakston Bitter together with Carlsberg lager and Woodpecker cider. Sandwiches, hot soup and light snacks are only available to pre-booked angling, walking, birdwatching and windsurfing parties. Children are not permitted in the bars, but a front beer garden is provided.

Opening times Monday to Saturday are 12 noon to 3 pm and 7 pm to 11 pm. Sunday hours are 12 noon to 2.30 pm and 7 pm to 10.30 pm.

Telephone: 01924 862370.

10

How to get there: The inn is in the hamlet of Wintersett south of Crofton near Wakefield.

Parking: Park in the car park opposite the inn.

Length of the walk: 1 mile. OS Map Landranger series 111 (inn GR 382157).

An easy circuit of the newly formed and planted 78 acres Anglers Lake – an outstanding transformation from pit to parkland.

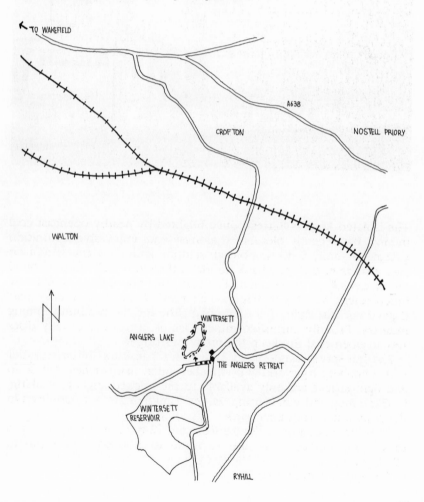

The Walk

Turn right from the inn and walk on for 100 yards (roadside nature reserve). At the bend, turn right again along a quiet lane for a further 300 yards and follow the sign on your right to 'Anglers Country Park'. On a gradually descending path continue to the lakeside and follow the shoreline in a clockwise direction, returning to the inn on the route by which you came.

Watch out for the newly established pols (wildlife ponds), an excellent bird hide, grebes, moorhens, swans and other rarer fowl and a 22,000 strong contingent of brown and rainbow trout that attract a sizeable sprouting of rods.

Other local attractions: Fly fishing, birdwatching and windsurfing, and more extended walks in Haw Park Wood.

Birstall
The Black Bull

This retiring beast vies with its neighbouring church for antiquity. More properly known as the Ye Olde Black Bull whose history begins with the Augustinian Order of Friars around AD 1200, the inn is low beamed and dark oaked, an unhurried and a relaxing venue for enjoying hearty meals and fine ales.

Home-made starters such as pea and ham soup and farmhouse broth prelude robust special menus which typically include mouclad (mussels in a brandy, cream and curry sauce), lobster thermidore, Dover sole, a range of grilled steaks, steak and Guinness pie and spaghetti carbonara. Traditional roast lunches are available on Sundays. Children are welcome for meals. Three excellent hand-pulled bitter beers are on tap – Trophy, Boddingtons and Castle Eden – together with Heineken, Stella and Gold lagers and Guinness and Murphy's stouts. Upstairs, the inn has a fascinating function room – a former centre of local jurisprudence. The last trial was held here in 1839 but the old courtroom has been strictly preserved. The dock and the big wigs' podium still survive.

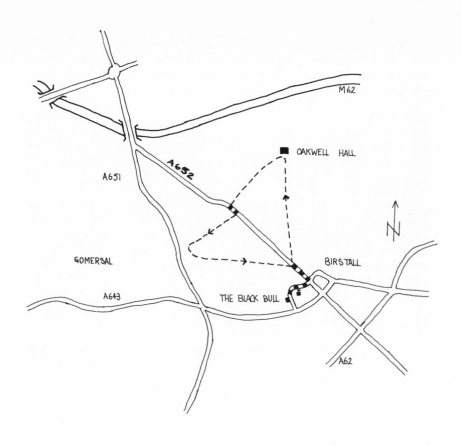

The inn is open from Monday to Saturday 12 noon to 3 pm and 6.30 pm to 11 pm. Sunday hours are 12 noon to 3 pm and 7 pm to 10.30 pm.
Telephone: 01274 873039.

How to get there: The inn is in Birstall, behind the parish church of St Peter, just off the A652 (west of the town centre; take junction 27 from the M62).

Parking: Park in the inn car park to the rear or on street.

Length of the walk: 2 miles. OS Map Landranger series 140 (inn GR 218262).

An easy field trip to Oakworth Hall – which is a manor house furnished in 1690s style; the former home of the Batt family described as 'Fieldhead' in Charlotte Brontë's novel 'Shirley'. There is also a visitor centre, arboretum and cafe – admission charge to Hall.

The Walk

Turn left from the inn and go right, past the church, turning left by the pond. Go right to the road and turn left. Opposite Monk Ings (signposted) turn right along the waymarked footpath, and walk on to Oakworth Hall. It is well worth a visit and you may wish to spend some time here.

Leaving the Hall, take the right footpath fork, following the distinctive sandy track to the road. Turn left, cross the road, and 100 yards before The Scotland pub, turn right, following the marked footpath up a gentle gradient to the top. Go left between buildings and go left again (no sign), heading towards a bungalow. Turn right by the side of a football pitch to a gate, go through the gap and walk on towards the next gate and bungalows. Turn right, away from the gate and find a gap in the fence, turning left to the overgrown churchyard. Follow the path to the road and turn right back to the inn.

Other local attractions: Red House, Gomersal (built in 1660 it recreates a family home of the 1830s – further connections with the Brontës – admission free).

Norwood Green
The Old White Beare

Run up the colours for a historic inn that has a heart of oak, and pipe me aboard a joyously cared for flagship of England's licensed trade, constructed in 1593 using timbers from Sir Francis Drake's Armada warship the *Old White Beare*. Garlanded in ivy and beautifully aged, this keel beamed pub stirs patriotic emotions, its linenfold panelled bar and beeswaxed settles celebrating Britannia's timeless best. The inn has a main, twin decked bar decorated with jugs, carvings, brasses, period prints and intriguing ships' manifests, a cosy open fired snug (spy the sailors' initials?) unusually furnished with butcher's block tables, and an equally characterful children's room.

Home-made food served at lunchtimes only would grace the admiral's table. Changed daily, the fare includes soup, beef in red wine, moussaka, chicken in white wine, sweet and sour pork, plaice with a prawn and mushroom filling, grilled steaks and gammon, jam roly poly and treacle sponge. Besides the grog, drinkers can choose from hand-pulled Castle Eden and Trophy bitters (together with a guest beer), Stella Artois and Heineken lagers, Woodpecker and Dry Blackthorn ciders, draught Guinness and draught Murphy's stout

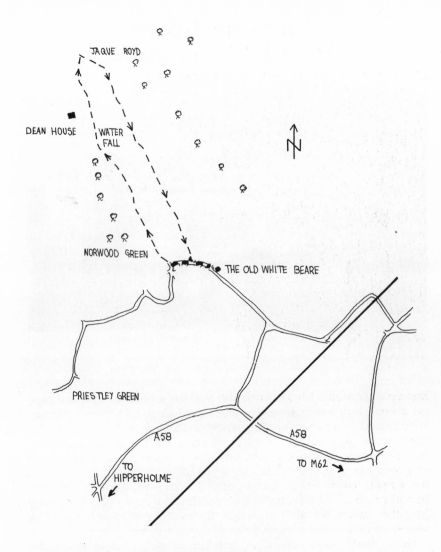

The inn has a pleasant beer garden to the rear and is open from Monday to Saturday 11.30 to 3 pm and 6 pm to 11 pm. Sunday hours are 12 noon to 3 pm and 7 pm to 10.30 pm.
Telephone: 01274 676645.

How to get there: The inn is in the village of Norwood Green to the north-east of Halifax, some 3 miles west of junction 26 on the M62.

Parking: Park in the inn car park.

Length of the walk: 2 miles. OS Map Landranger series 104 (inn GR 140270).

An easy dawdle along trackways visiting ancient farmsteads and a waterfall. The last vestiges of the area's industrial past can be seen in a lone smoking chimney. The peace and solitude defy the proximity of the towns.

The Walk
Turn right from the inn along the street, and pass St George's church. Go round the bend and walk on to the next bend – Norwood Green Hill – and turn right opposite Chatsworth House along a track (footpath plate missing).

Continue towards power lines. Go under, keeping wallside, and where the wall ends, turn left diagonally downhill across the meadow towards woodland. Turn right along the bank at the top of the ravine. Drop down to inspect the waterfall – evidence of old mill works here – and climb the bank, going left to a stile. Cross, walk on with garages to your left and continue uphill to Jaque Royd Farm. Turn right, following a well defined track into Norwood Green. Turn left to the inn.

Other local attractions: Shibden Hall 2 miles to the west (15th century hall set in 90 acres of parkland – boating, miniature railway, play areas – furnished rooms and horse drawn carriages).

Heath
The King's Arms

An atoll of green, Heath casts a grassy snook at the industrialisation all around. An elevated village of elegant mansions and cottages encircled by acres of lawn, Wakefield's premier conservation area stands aloof from the nearby city, offering unbridled opportunities for walking and one of the most characterful inns in West Yorkshire. The 17th century King's Arms – all flagstones, wainscotting and gaslights – stands a full toss from Heath Hall. It has three intimate bars log-flamed in winter, one sporting a genuine Yorkshire range, and a fine collection of bygones. The ghost of Lady Bolles (only part of her remains were laid to rest in Heath – her intestines were left in Ledsham!) adds to the atmosphere.

The inn serves both bar and restaurant meals lunchtimes and evenings. Casual diners can choose from hot roast of the day, omelettes, lasagne, beef pie, vegetarian bake or specials such as game casserole, steak in ale or black pudding in mustard sauce. Formal trenchermen with an appetite for the Jacobean ambience of the restaurant can select from a wide range of dishes including beef

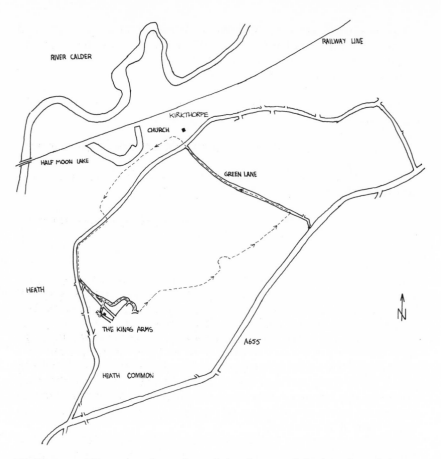

RIVER CALDER

RAILWAY LINE

KIRKTHORPE

CHURCH

HALF MOON LAKE

GREEN LANE

HEATH

THE KINGS ARMS

A655

HEATH COMMON

N

Wellington, T bone steak, veal svedoise, breast of duck, sole or lobster thermidore, followed by an Italian temptation – an oven baked trifle consisting of liqueur soaked sponge topped with creme patissiere, meringue and dimpled cherries and almonds. The liquid fare is equally enticing, past guest beers like Dreadnought, Whitby Wobble and Force Nine vying for popularity alongside resident brews – hand-pulled Clarks and Tetleys bitters and Timothy Taylor's Landlord. Stella Artois and Heineken lagers, Strongbow and Woodpecker ciders and Guinness are also available.

The King's Arms has an ample rear patio which is ideal for summer barbecues. The inn also boasts the largest beer garden in the world! In fine weather, empty glasses can be recovered over a mile from the bar on the adjacent Heath Common.

Opening times are from Monday to Saturday, 11 am to 3 pm and 6 pm to 11 pm. Sunday hours are 12 noon to 3 pm and 7 pm to 10.30 pm. Children are welcome for meals.
Telephone: 01924 377527.

How to get there: The inn is in the village of Heath, off the A655, south-east of Wakefield.

Parking: Park opposite the inn or in the large visitor car park nearby.

Length of the walk: 1½ miles. OS Map Landranger series 104 (inn GR 357200).

A short, surprisingly rural orbit of wide vistas, discovering the most superior of Georgian villages and a swan paddled (half) moon.

The Walk
Turn right from the inn past King's Arms Cottages, and turn right again along an access road to entrance gates and a wall. Follow the wall round to the right passing several mullioned cottages to find a marked footpath near Manor House Nursing Home. Turn left along the footpath, ascending between thorn hedges. At the top of the track, go right through a gate and cross a field, taking a diagonal right to a kissing gate. Turn left, following field boundaries for about ½ mile to join a track. Turn left and continue to the crest, noticing the river Calder in the distance. (It is the most mucked about watercourse in Yorkshire! Its waters will soon be diverted to make way for Europe's biggest landfill operation.)

Walk on to the road and the hamlet of Kirkthorpe. Cross the road and follow the winding access, turning left on a woodland path opposite Warmfield House. (Notice Half Moon Lake nature reserve in the valley to your right. Tampering with nature is as old as the hills. The lake was created when the river was elbowed aside to accommodate the railway.) Walk on and continue uphill to the road. Turn right, following the estate boundary wall into Heath.

Other local attractions: Heath Common, Heath Hall, the church of St. Peter in Kirkthorpe and the Welbeck Landfill visitor centre (wherein are displayed the plans for the river diversion).

Bingley
The Old White Horse

The riverside Old White Horse breathes antiquity, a veil of whitewash sprucing its weathered stones. Built on the site of a 14th century hostelry reputed to have been founded by the Knights Hospitallers of St John, this former coaching inn echoes the spirit of old England – wainscotting, drunken beams, open fireplaces and its reputation for the pleasurable things in life hardly changed in 300 years '. . . it is by far the best place in Bingley to repair to . . . its wenches being comely, the steak and kidney pudding most substantial and the ale cool and foaming.'

Although modest, the modern victuals are nutritious and reasonably priced, and the giant Yorkshire puddings, omelettes and home-made curries are particularly recommended. A range of vegetarian dishes is also available. Children are welcome for meals. Pride of the pumps are hand-pulled Bass, Worthington and Stones bitters, Bass Light Mild, Caffrey's Irish Ale. Carling Black Label, and Grolsch lagers, Autumn Gold and Dry Blackthorn ciders and draught Guinness are the alternative brews.

The inn is open from Monday to Thursday 12 noon to 3 pm and 5.30 pm to 11 pm. Friday and Saturday openings are from 11 am to 11 pm. Sunday hours are 12 noon to 3 pm and 7.30 pm to 10.30 pm. Telephone: 01274 563236.

How to get there: The inn is in Bingley, at the junction of Millgate and the Keighley Road A650.

Parking: The inn has no parking to speak of. Park on street beyond the church. Pay and display facilities are available in the town centre.

Length of the walk: 1½ miles. OS Map Landranger series 104 (inn GR 106394).

A riverside dawdle – ideal for a hot day.

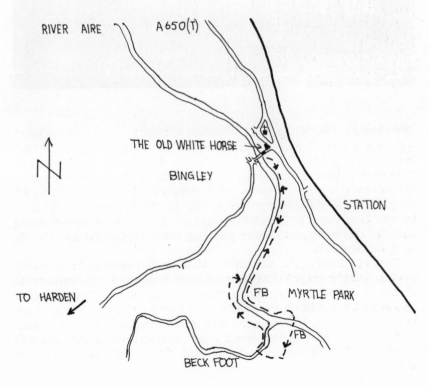

The Walk

Turn right from the inn and turn immediately right again down Millgate. Do not cross the bridge, but go left through the archway 'River Walk'. Walk on the riverbank passing a footbridge and enter Myrtle Park, continuing to the next footbridge. Turn right, crossing the river Aire and passing allotment gardens to a narrow road. Go right into the hamlet of Beck Foot and bide awhile by a graceful little bridge built in 1723 for £10.

Cross the bridge and go right through a gap in the wall, swinging left uphill past the river frontage of a house. Enter woodland and fork right, dropping down to the river and the footbridge. Cross and turn left back to the inn.

Other local attractions: Five Rise Locks on the Leeds and Liverpool Canal, 1 mile to the north.

Leeds
Whitelock's

In a world where interior pub designs rarely outlast the beer mats, Whitelock's, in Turk's Head Yard, Leeds, has a timeless charm. Squeezed into a backwater alley off busy Briggate, this compact inn, always busy and extremely popular with students, businessmen and shoppers alike, was founded as the Turk's Head in 1715, taking its more popular name from a family who held the licence for 90 years. Untouched since 1886, when it was waitered by a team of dwarfs, its stained glass, tiles and brasswork have since acquired the patina and aroma of smoked ham. A unique feature of the pub is its long muralled yard, colourfully illuminated with rustic scenes and set out with barrel tables and benches. A further attraction is the comparatively new, chip off the old Whitelock's, top bar.

There is a taste of the good old days about the bulldog British menu. Beef and dripping sandwiches, bubble and squeak and meat and potato pie could inspire a Churchillian speech in the House of Commons . . . and that's just the bar food. Come early, grab a white cloth-laid table and enjoy Yorkshire pudding (with gravy which you could swab by the glassful), whitebait, Scotch pot (beef coated with

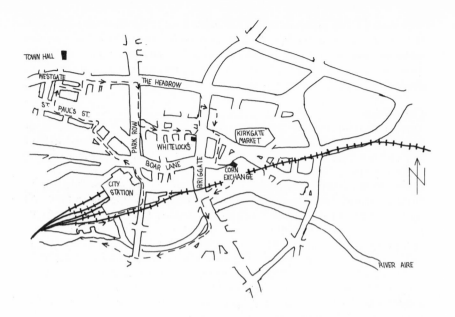

onions and mushrooms and simmered in bitter), lamb chops, T bone steak and seafood pie. And to the strains of 'Land of Hope and Glory' you must finish with jam roly poly! Sundays see a clearing of the decks for traditional roast lunches. Children are welcome for meals. Amongst the liquid refreshments, hand-pulled tartan brews predominate – Younger Scotch Bitter, Younger No.3, IPA, 80/- and McEwan lager alongside Theakston Bitter, Becks lager, Dry Blackthorn and Autumn Gold ciders and draught Guinness.

Whitelock's is open from Monday to Saturday – 11 am to 11 pm. Sunday hours are 12 noon to 3 pm and 7.30 pm to 10.30 pm.

Telephone: 0113 245 3950.

How to get there: Whitelock's is in Turk's Head Yard off Briggate (near Marks and Spencers), Leeds.

Parking: As with all large city centres, parking is strictly limited at peak periods. For a fee, facilities are available adjacent to the West Yorkshire Playhouse at Quarry Hill and on cleared ground south of Boar Lane.

Length of the walk: 2 miles. OS Map Landranger series 104 (inn GR 303335).

Pocketfuls of loot and credit cards are an impediment to this interesting city amble. Do not allow shopping to interfere with your exploration of Yorkshire's premier centre for commerce and culture. You will encounter a dazzling array of architectural styles and civic monuments. To seasoned Loiners used to dead dogs and soapsuds, the backwater renaissance of river and canal is surprising and exciting stuff.

The Walk

Turn right from the inn down the yard and turn left along Briggate for 200 yards. Turn right across the road and enter the Victorian Quarter (formerly an open street, now magnificently covered with a stained glass structure). Go next right opposite the fountain and walk on down Fish Street. Go left and right along Central Road and cross Duncan Street, taking a peep at another typical old Leeds yard to the right of The Duncan pub. Turn left and cross Call Lane to the Corn Exchange – a unique creation of architect Cuthbert Brodrick completed as a grain mart in 1863 (now converted to house fashionable shops and cafes). Walk on towards the cupolaed building – another historical landmark – the White Cloth Hall erected in 1775 for the sale of cloth. Turn right to The Calls and go next left over the river on Leeds Bridge. Swing right, walk on down Water Lane to the side of the Old Red Lion and join the new riverside promenade. Continue to the Victoria Bridge.

Cross the road and continue along Water Lane, forking right on Canal Wharf. Arc right by the Canal Office over the canal bridge, pass a berth and go left under the arch of the viaduct, entering Granary Wharf and the Dark Arches. A remarkable feat of engineering allows the river to flow underneath the city at this point; the resultant caverns are imaginatively used for retailing. Turn right, crossing the river to Bishopgate Street. Turn left to City Square whose civic island is graced with statuary. Go left along Quebec Street, turn right and then left down St. Paul's Street admiring yet another architectural show piece, the Moorish styled St. Paul's House built in 1878 for John Barren the first Leeds clothing manufacturer. Turn right down St. Paul's Place, cut through the garden and turn right and left to Westgate.

The most impressive civic building in England greets you – another tour-de-force by Brodrick. Turn right and opposite the cenotaph, turn right along Park Row. Go next left into the pedestrian precinct, weaving right and left to the Lands Lane concourse. Turn right and later sharp left into Turk's Head Yard. Walk on to the inn.

Other local attractions: Leeds City Art Gallery and Museum and the Royal Armouries Collection (to be rehoused from London into a purpose built exhibition complex near the river).

Haworth
The Black Bull

A den for Branwell Brontë's orgiastic encounters with strong drink and opium (it eased the pain of tuberculosis), the Black Bull is as much a part of the Brontë legend as the novels themselves. At the crest of Haworth's rakish cobbled street, within staggering distance of the famous parsonage, the inn is a compulsive stop on the pilgrimage tour. Despite its modernity and plushness, the inn emits the indefinable character of a roué. Is it the extended Sunday opening, Branwell's preserved parlour chair, the evocative Brontë prints or the reputed presence of a ghost in a polka dot skirt?

Matching the literary sinews of *Wuthering Heights* and the rest, the Black Bull presents a heroically Yorkshire menu. Try the Yorkshire pudding, corned beef hash, steak and ale pie, home-made beef stew and dumplings, game pie, hot black pudding and apple, old fashioned chicken crumble or the venison sausage, followed by bread and butter pudding, treacle sponge or spotted dick. Cream teas, pastries, gateaux, teacakes and scones are also available and children are welcome for meals. A selection of hand-pulled real ales are on tap – Timothy Taylor, Marston Pedigree, Flowers and Boddington bitters – supplemented

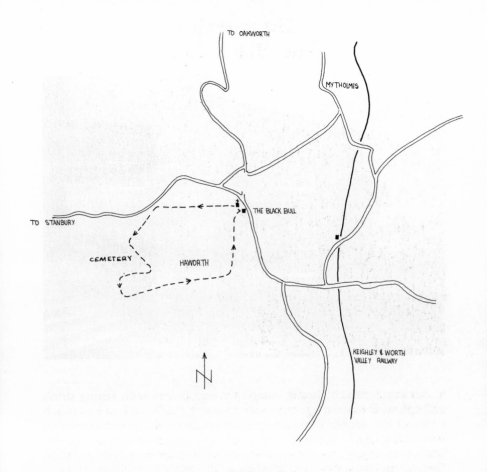

by a guest beer every fortnight and Heineken and Stella Artois lagers, draught Guinness and Murphy's stouts and Strongbow and Wood-pecker ciders.

The Black Bull has 3 letting bedrooms and an outside seating area and is open from Monday to Saturday 11 am to 11 pm. Sunday hours are 12 noon to 10.30 pm (between 3 pm and 7 pm, intoxicating liquor is only available to diners).

Telephone: 01535 642249.

How to get there: The inn is at the top of Main Street in the village of Haworth.

Parking: Park in the inn car park (although this entails negotiating the cobbles which may be thronged with visitors). Pay and display facilities are available close by. These are well signposted from Sun Street which is contiguous with Main Street.

Length of the walk: 1½ miles. OS Map Landranger series 104 (inn GR 030373).

A short and easy amble to the inspirational Haworth moors . . . there will be adequate time for exploring the village.

The Walk
Turn immediately left from the inn, and climb the steps to St. Michael and All Angels church. The Reverend Patrick Brontë was the incumbent here. See the ranks of gravestones. What a forbidding place for 6 young souls! Go right, to the back of the church, and turn left on a signposted path passing the Brontë Parsonage Museum (entrance fee). Continue through a gate onto open fields. Cross, and at the road turn left, forking left after 50 yards down Cemetery Road. Walk on the right hand verge footpath. Turn left opposite the layby near the cemetery on a signposted track, following the graveyard wall round to the right. On reaching a stone marker numbered 9, go sharp left on a diagonal track to the road. Cross, and follow a sign to Haworth Church, dropping down past a cottage to an intersection of routes. Notice here that some of the direction signs are in Japanese! Turn left back to the church and the inn.

Other local attractions: Haworth shops and the Keighley and Worth Valley Railway (steam hauled trains).

Newmillerdam
The Dam Inn

At the gateway to a country park, this former coaching inn is tailor made for a pub walk, its stone clad exterior betraying little of the opulence inside. But the chintz, comfortable seating and platter sized meals do not inspire the idle leg, so complete your tramping first!

Spacious, relaxing and stylishly modern with a patina of antiquity, the Dam has a deserved reputation for both bar snacks and more formal meals. Casual diners with an eye for a lakeside stroll can select from a varied menu which includes blackboard specials and standard steak and kidney pie, lasagne, roast chicken, casseroles and jumbo Whitby haddock delivered fresh daily. For those whose exercise is restricted to plumbing the depths of an armchair, the menu of the Toby Carving Room is tempting and unusual, offering mushroom coriander, spicy prawn combo, herb crepes, feta cheese and tuna salad and capellelli carbonara as well as roasts. Tapside, Stones, Worthington Bitter and Caffrey's Irish Ale, Tennent's and Carling Black Label lagers, Taunton Autumn Gold cider and Guinness are available. Children are welcome for meals and pre-booked parties are catered for.

The inn is open from Monday to Saturday 11 am to 3 pm and 5.30 pm to 11 pm. Sunday hours are 12 noon to 3 pm and 7 pm to 10.30 pm.
Telephone: 01924 255625.

How to get there: The inn is in Newmillerdam on the A61 Barnsley Road near Wakefield.

Parking: Park in the inn car park. Alternative facilities are available close by.

Length of the walk: 1¾ miles. OS Map Landranger series 110 (inn GR 333158).

An easy lakeside saunter you could accomplish in slippers. There are mallard, grebe, swans and occasional sparrowhawks hereabouts, but the audacious coots are the undoubted stars of the show. Their text book timidity vanishes at the sight of a loaf . . . but watch your fingers! This walk is suitable for children and wheelchair users.

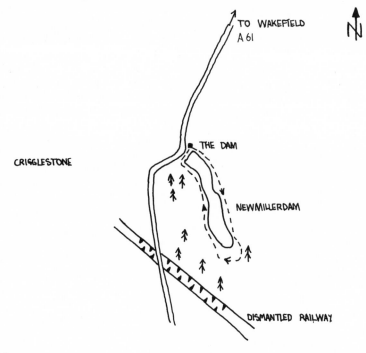

The Walk

Begin the walk opposite the inn, starting from East Lodge. Walk on, passing a boathouse (built in 1827 as a fishing and shooting lodge). At the end of the lake, fork left on an ascending track into woodland. Turn right over a bridged stream and turn right again dropping down to the lake. Go left to West Lodge. Turn right along Barnsley Road to the inn.

Other local attractions: Sandal Castle, Anglers Lake (windsurfing) and Wooley Edge (viewpoint).

Thorner
The Fox

A West Yorkshire 'Best Kept Village' award winner, Thorner is blessed with three pubs. The Fox is the most traditional, an unspoilt and a relaxing venue for discussing the price of a pint.

Reynard's taxidermal squint eyes every room. Besides the hunting trophies, there are also fine collections of plates and photographs of local scenes. Served Monday to Saturday in the lounge, tap room and cosy snug under the banner 'All Home Made', the seasonally adapted menu features dishes such as farmhouse soup, Yorkshire puddings, quiche, fisherman's pie, meat and potato pie, broccoli, sliced potato and cream cheese bake, chicken kiev and rhubarb crumble. Children are welcome for meals. The house hand-pulled ales are Tetley Bitter and Mild (plus a guest beer). The alternative brews are Castlemaine and Carlsberg lager, Gaymer's Olde English cider and draught Guinness. The inn has an attractive beer garden to the rear.

Opening times are from Monday to Saturday 11 am to 11 pm. Sunday hours are 12 noon to 3 pm and 7 pm to 10.30 pm.

Telephone: 0113 289 2489.

How to get there: The inn is on Main Street in the village of Thorner, north of Leeds.

Parking: Park in the inn car park.

Length of the walk: 2 miles. OS Map Landranger series 104 (inn GR 378404).

A grassy, all-ages rural stroll . . . watch out for foxes on the prowl . . . I was stalked by one . . . the pub has wallspace yet!

The Walk
Turn right from the pub along Main Street and go round the bend past St. Peter's Church. At the next bend, go left along the quiet road (Milner Lane) signposted to 'Scarcroft and Bardsey'. Turn right opposite the house known as Hawthorns and follow the waymarked footpath to 'Wothersome' over a stile. Go left of the telegraph pole and keep hedgeside to the next stile. Cross, and go straight forward, walking on a narrow plateau strip parallel to the valley of the beck to your left. Continue to the edge of a wood. Cross a stile into the wood and veer left, crossing a footbridge. Climb slightly and emerge from

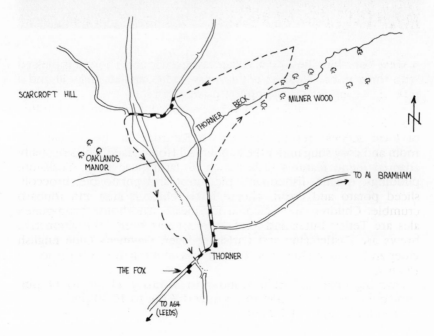

the trees, keeping fieldside and walking on to meet a track. Turn left down the track to a road junction.

Keep going forward, following the road signposted to 'Scarcroft'. Swing right past a farm, cross a bridge over a defunct railway and turn left along a road following the signpost to 'Ten Hill Computer Systems'. Turn left after 50 yards down the side of East Lodge along the Leeds Country Way. Swing left to a stile, cross and go down the centre of the field to a kissing gate. Go through, walk on, in the ditch, to the next stile, cross and continue into Thorner. Go left and then right at the road, back to the pub.

Other local attractions: Bramham Park, a Queen Anne house built 1698-1710, set in formal grounds with monuments, temples and follies and gardens inspired by those at Versailles.

Jackson Bridge
The White Horse Inn

Yorkshire bloodstock, more shire than Shergar, the White Horse Inn snuggles in the hollow of a mill beck. Famous TV local of 'Last of the Summer Wine' chums Compo, Foggy and Clegg, this homely inn could well have been stage struck, but like Nora Batty's broom it is short on ceremony, offering one of the warmest welcomes in West Yorkshire. It also has a real piano! Knees-up night is Saturday.

Served in interconnecting rooms, wallpapered with over 500 photographs of the stars, bar meals are generous and lusty. Top of the bill is Grandma Batty's Yorkshire Pudding. Steak and kidney pudding, beef casserole, sirloin steak and a selection of hot sandwiches play distinguished supporting roles. Special dishes are available on request and children are welcome for meals. The excellent hand-pulled ales are Stones and Riding bitters and Bass Light and Bass Mild. Guinness, Beamish Stout and Carling Black Label lager are the alternative brews. Teas and coffees are served daily from 9 am. The inn has 5 en-suite letting bedrooms. Be assured – Compo is barred!

The inn is open for alcoholic drinks from Monday to Saturday 11 am to 11 pm. Sunday hours are 12 noon to 3 pm and 7 pm to 10.30 pm.

Telephone: 01484 683940.

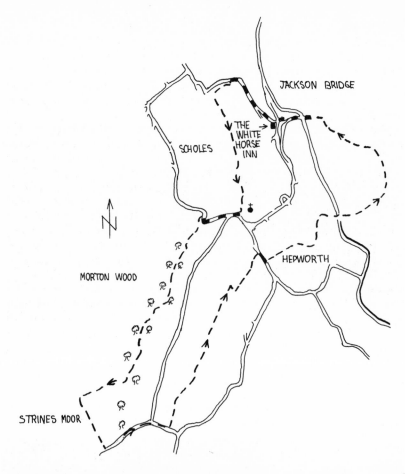

How to get there: The inn is in the hamlet of Jackson Bridge, just off the A616 (Sheffield to Huddersfield Road) near Holmfirth.

Parking: Parking is limited, both in front of and opposite the inn. Spaces are available on street close by.

Length of the walk: 4 miles. OS Map Landranger series 110 (inn GR 164074).

Away from major settlements and highways, peace reigns supreme on this gentle streamside and meadows ramble. A little road walking is involved, but even on a Saturday afternoon in the height of summer, traffic is very light.

38

The Walk

Turn left from the inn uphill on the footway above the mill pond. Go round the bend at the top to the next bend and turn left by the access to Lee Mills Industrial Park, following the marked footpath. Walk on between dry-stone walls, heading for a distant steeple. Swing right downhill to fishponds and go left over the footbridge, ascending right and left to the church.

Turn right on the road downhill to the bend and take the marked footpath to your left, mounting a stile and walking on a meandering path streamside for about a mile. Climb several steps heading away from the stream to your right and go sharp left and left again walking away from a huddle of cottages uphill. Keep straight on over 3 fields, dropping down to a road. Turn left on the road, passing the end of Dean Lane. Look out for a tubular gate to your left and go left over a wall stile onto a soccer pitch (unmarked public right of way). Head for the corner, and walk on, crossing several fields on a well defined footpath. At the last field before reaching the farmyard, go sharp right by the wall and find a wall stile in the corner. Cross and go left into the village of Hepworth. Turn right for a short distance, and go left near to telegraph pole 7, following a yellow arrow head marker down steps. Nearing the bottom of the meadow, turn right over a stile and go left, swinging right uphill to the road. Cross and take the track signposted 'Kirklees Way', arcing left back into Jackson Bridge. Keep left at South View and continue forward down Earl Street back to the inn.

Other local attractions: Holmfirth – TV location for the series 'Last of the Summer Wine' and home to Bamforth's Postcard Museum.

Burley Woodhead
The Hermit

A former refuge of drovers, the roadside Hermit has a hillside perch, commanding eyrie views from its comfortable back bar. Small and snug, the inn is presided over by a portrait of Job Senior, singer, soothsayer and hermit who would have appreciated the inn's enduring appeal to the windswept.

Walkers, cyclists and grouse beaters are admirably catered for in a wholesome and restorative menu which includes home-made soup, Yorkshire puddings, chicken and mushroom pie, cheesy crust veggie pie and daily specials such as meat and potato pie, Lancashire hot pot, liver, bacon and sausage casserole, beef stew and dumplings and braised rabbit. A quartet of hand-pulled bitter beers – John Smith's, Directors, Magnet and Tetley and Ruddles bitters (together with Guinness and Beamish Stout, Carlsberg, Foster's lager and Dry Blackthorn cider) complete the antidote for exposure. Children are welcome for meals and the Hermit has a terraced beer garden to the rear.

The inn is open from Monday to Saturday 11.30 am to 3 pm and 5.30 pm to 11 pm. Sunday hours are from 12 noon to 3 pm and 7 pm to 10.30 pm. Customers can enjoy uninterrupted opening during Bank Holidays.

Telephone: 01943 863204.

How to get there: The inn is in the hamlet of Burley Woodhead on the edge of Rombalds and Burley Moors, south of Burley in Wharfedale off the A65.

Parking: Park in the inn car park. (Customers should be cautious in using the front entrance. Access is via the roadway. A tight bend and the absence of a footway makes the short walk to the entrance potentially dangerous. Safeguard children.)

Length of the walk: 4½ miles. OS Map Landranger series 104 (inn GR 154448).

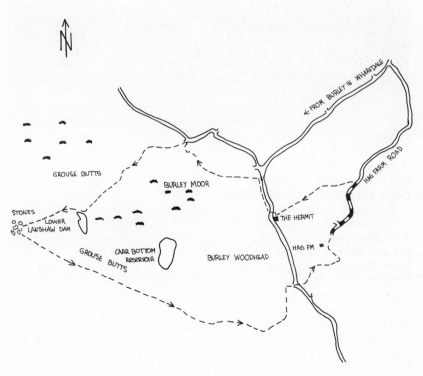

A curse for agoraphobics – wheeling panoramas in this realm of the grouse and the curlew make this a giddy and exhilarating walk. Come in search of cairns entrenchments, strangely inscribed stones and solitude . . . but avoid wearing a feather in your cap on August 12! Three steep ascents are involved.

The Walk

Turn right from the inn using the roadside footway and walk downhill for 200 yards. Turn left opposite Moor Lane End and follow a footpath sign through a gate onto Burley Moor. Walk uphill and at the crest veer right on a track through heather, keeping to the edge of a crag. Drop down to a stream. Cross. Ascend the hill and go left following the course of a narrow valley. Guided by white marker posts (I've put them there specially!) and steering between Lower Lanshaw Dam to your left and a pile of stones on the horizon to your right, continue. Turn left at the stones along an access track.

Gradually descend with Carr Bottom Reservoir to your left. Go through a gate, and 100 yards before the house with green barge boards, turn left, dropping down, veering right and going through a gate to a walled path. Walk on for a short distance, crossing a beck to an access road. Turn right and cross the main road, following a marked footpath downhill for 100 yards. Turn left down steps and continue on a wriggling path beckside to a wall in the dip. Turn left towards Hag Farm. Bear right away from the farm and walk on Hagg Farm Road past Primrose Cottage. (The next change of direction is tricky – eyes peeled for an unmarked footpath to the left. It is hard by an old tree, 200 yards before the large house with the tennis court.) Turn left over a stile and steer left over two fields towards a small copse. Go right through a white kissing gate and ascend to the inn.

Other local attractions: Otley (market and river attractions including boating and fishing).

Ledsham
The Chequers

A cosy and an immensely quiet little inn winking out from a mantilla of ivy, the Chequers has been the centre of village life for centuries. Low-beamed, wainscotted and log flickered in winter, the inn has a Pickwickian charm, enhanced by brasses and rustic prints.

Standard bar meals such as York ham, smoked salmon scramble, lasagne and a variety of crusty sandwiches are supplemented by daily specials which include fresh fish and game in season. Evening diners can enjoy the first floor intimacy of the 32 cover restaurant, Friday and Saturday evenings only, whose varied menu offers roast duckling, beef stroganoff, red mullet provencal and curried nut loaf. Children are welcome for meals. The bar-top line up fields hand-pulled Theakston, Younger, Younger No.3 and John Smith's bitters, McEwans, Becks and Carlsberg lagers, Guinness, and Strongbow cider.

The Chequers has an excellent beer garden. Alas, the inn is closed on Sundays. We can blame drunken farm workers for this lamentable state of affairs. Years ago, they verbally abused the estate owner on her way to church, and the towels have been draped on the Sabbath ever since. The rest of the week, opening times are from Monday to Friday 11 am to 3 pm and 5.30 pm to 11 pm; on Saturday, the inn is open all day.

Telephone: 01977 683135.

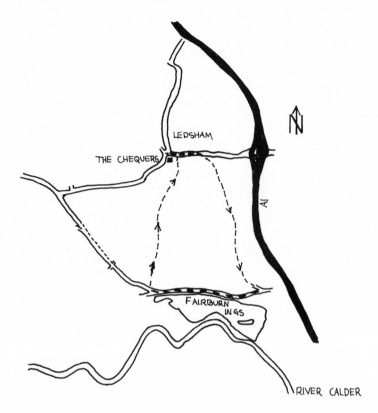

How to get there: The inn is in the village of Ledsham near the A1 south-east of Garforth.

Parking: Park in the inn car park.

Length of the walk: 3½ miles. OS Map Landranger series 105 (inn GR 456298).

An easy field edge hike, enjoying Nature at her adaptable best. You will have an opportunity to visit Fairburn Ings – a remarkable floodbowl – a consequence of mining extraction and one of the premier sites in England for migratory birds.

The Walk

From the inn, turn right along Claypit Lane, past All Saints' Church (interesting monument to Lady Mary Bolles whose ghost is said to haunt the bar of the King's Arms, Heath – walk number 5). Continue round the bend and proceed out of the village to a second bend. Proceed without changing direction along a marked footpath. Keeping to the edge of a beech wood, emerge into a field. Cross, steering left to a stile about 80 yards from the field corner. Mount two stiles in quick succession and walk uphill, following a rough line of brambles to the crest (to the right, in the valley, you will see Fairburn Ings.) Cross a stile and continue along the perimeter of private woodland (quaintly marked with signs 'Alarm Mines' . . . 'It saves the courts a great deal of trouble,' says the gamekeeper).

Mount a further stile and pass Palmerston Lodge on a downhill track, bearing left by bungalows to the road. Turn right. (Ornothologists, up scopes here! Dozens of resident and migratory waterfowl can be observed from bankside hides. Birdwatchers turn left down a snicket between the houses at the bottom of the hill, allowing an extra 1½ hours on your day.) Walkers march on down the road, forking right after a mile along Back Newton Lane. After a few strides, turn right along the Newfield Lane bridleway, skirting the edge of a plantation back into Ledsham.

Other local attractions: All Saints' Church and Fairburn Ings nature reserve.

Tong
The Greyhound

At deep square-leg, this cosy, yet fashionable little inn, keeps a bailside vigil. The home of two cricket teams, the mid-week resort of business customers and an increasingly popular destination for walkers, the Greyhound is in the lofty village of Tong, in the embattled green belt between Leeds and Bradford. Low slung beams, stone flagged floors, a long case clock and a magnificent collection of Toby jugs give the inn a distinctive personality, enlivened on summer's evenings when stumps are drawn.

The Greyhound's semi circular bar is segregated for bar and restaurant meals. Daily blackboard bar specials such as crepes, seafood platter, savoury pies and fresh pasta are supplemented by a range of salads, sandwiches and toasties. The standard restaurant fare is extensive and ambitious. Starters include mushrooms stuffed with crabmeat, breaded and served with nutmeg sauce, smoked salmon and barbecued spare ribs. Main courses offer chateaubriand in Madeira sauce, lamb escalopes with redcurrants, pork marsala, duckling, sautéed chicken with tarragon, Dover sole and a selection of exotic fish and shellfish served on a bed of saffron rice. Seasonal twelfth men include meringues, flambéd pancakes, fresh fruit compotes, fruit pies and peaches in brandy. Children are welcome for meals. The liquid choices are hand-pulled Tetleys Bitter and Mild, Burton Bitter, Lowenbrau, Castlemaine and Skol lagers, and Olde English cider. The Greyhound has little need for a beer garden. If you are not deterred by the highly unlikely sound of leather on glass, there are ample acres close by.

The inn is open from Monday to Saturday 11.30 am to 3 pm and 5.30 pm to 11 pm. Sunday hours are 12 noon to 3 pm and 7 pm to 10.30 pm.

Telephone: 0113 285 2427.

How to get there: The inn is in the village of Tong, twixt Leeds and Bradford.

Parking: Park in the inn car park.

Length of the walk: 3½ miles. OS Map Landranger series 104 (inn GR 222306).

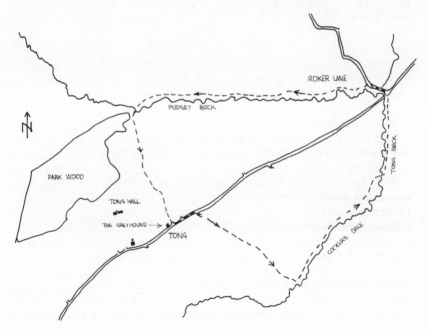

A generally easy amble on ancient trackways (one steep climb at the end) through Yorkshire's least known dale. It struggles valiantly to overcome continuing attempts at despoliation.

The Walk

Turn left from the inn and walk on the roadside footpath past Manor Farm. Turn right, following a public footpath signposted 'Farnley Park'. Drop downhill with a gas installation to your left and turn left over a stile following the waymarked 'Leeds Country Way' along the banks of the Tong Beck through Cockers Dale. Go right across a footbridge after ½ mile and continue left to Tong Lane. Cross the road and go left down Roker Lane, past the mill. Turn left after 20 yards along a marked footpath and follow the Pudsey Beck upstream, crossing the edge of a golf course to a metal footbridge. Turn left up a steep hill and continue to the crest and Keeper Lane (to the right is the impressive Tong Hall). Turn right to the inn, passing the restored pinfold (a pound for stray animals) on the roadside.

Other local attractions: Village church of St. James (1727), Tong Hall (1702) and Tong Garden Centre.

Sowerby
The Travellers Rest

A motorist's labyrinth ensures a splendid isolation for this moor top inn so mark the compass well. But wanderers despair not. Offering panoramic views, real ale and an adventurous menu running to over 80 dishes, deviations are soon forgotten.

Indulgence is the theme, so spoil yourself with three generous courses, either in the split level, quaintly alcoved bar or the 52 cover restaurant. The choice is impressive. Prepare the palate for new culinary encounters – frogs' legs, maigo (barbecued king prawns, spread with wholegrain mustard wrapped in bacon and oven baked), rabbit pie, carpetbagger (fillet steak stuffed with smoked oysters and coated with lobster sauce) and old smokie (a concoction of trout, mackerel and marlin). Traditionalists have the option of old favourites such as roast beef and Yorkshire pudding, beef cobbler, pan fried halibut and roast chicken and vegetarian alternatives are available. The reputation for amplitude is crowned by a succession of coup de grace

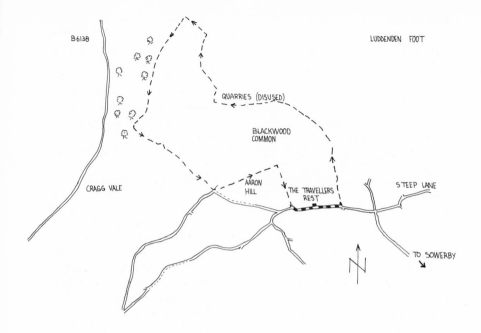

sweets – try the rigor mortis by raspberry. Children are welcome for meals. A trio of finely cellared hand-pulled ales, Tetley, Burton and Timothy Taylor's bitters vie for popularity alongside Falstaff Light Mild and Tetley Dark Mild. Labatts, Carlsberg, Castlemaine and Lowenbrau lagers, and Olde English cider are also on draught.

The inn is open from Monday to Sunday 12 noon to 3 pm and 7 pm to 12 midnight (11.30 pm on Sunday).

Telephone: 01422 832124.

How to get there: The inn is on the old Sowerby to Rochdale Roman road. Steep Lane, Sowerby is the official location, but the inn can be found about 1 mile west of the village. A lack of signposts underlines the worth of a map literate co-pilot.

Parking: Park in the inn car park.

Length of the walk: 4 miles. OS Map Landranger series 104 (inn GR 024236).

A moorland stroll to Cragg Vale – exhilarating views.

The Walk

Turn left from the inn and walk downhill on the road for 100 yards. Turn left onto a track by the cottage and continue to the intersection at Blackwood Common. Go left proceeding between a house and a quarry. Drop down swinging to your right. About 100 yards after the bend, fork left on a heather clogged track and arc right to a rusted gate. Go through, and without deviation continue forward in a ditch, following a wall. After 150 yards, turn left passing a barn and walk on, following a wall to the crest. Once you reach telegraph pole numbered H501/51, go left over a wall and walk on at the edge of the tree line – terrific views of Cragg Vale.

Continue for about ½ mile and opposite the gable end of a farmhouse, drop down to the right, then keep left on the crest path, wriggling uphill around scrub and boulders. Drop down again, swinging left at the sound of a stream, and follow the stream up (it accompanies the path between dry-stone walls). At the red gate, turn right onto an access road and climb to the intersection. Take the waymarked public footpath across the moorland to the left. Continue along the walled edge of a field and at the corner take the track to your right. Turn left on the road a short distance back to the inn.

Other local attractions: Cragg Vale.

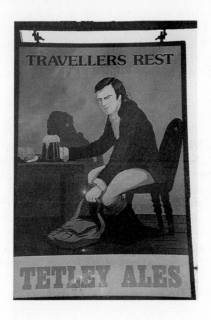

Wentbridge
The Bluebell

This former roost of outlaws and ne'er-do-wells once succoured saddle sore travellers on the worst stretch of road between London and Edinburgh. Today, a leaping viaduct relieves the strain and the old Bluebell is left to enjoy its declivity in peace.

Sensitively rebuilt in recent times and preserving its 17th century sign, the inn has lost none of its traditional atmosphere. Sporting as much oak as the Cutty Sark, the rugged bar and the adjacent lounge bear the unmistakable rodent imprint of Mouseman Thompson and the extensive menu, heralded by a deservedly popular giant haddock, matches the scene. Home-made steak and kidney pie, roast duckling and stew and dumplings are all available as standard meals supplemented by daily specials. Nut cutlets, broccoli and cheese bake and vegetable stroganoff provide the vegetarian alternative. Children are welcome for meals, and the inn has a garden area and an intimate upstairs function room. The beautifully adzed bar is graced by hand-pulled Tetley, Theakston and Timothy Taylor's bitters, Lowenbrau, Skol and Castlemaine lagers, Gaymer's Olde English cider, draught Guinness and draught wine.

The inn is open from Monday to Saturday 11.30 am to 3 pm and 6.30 pm to 11 pm. Sunday hours are from 12 noon to 3 pm and 7 pm to 10.30 pm.
Telephone: 01977 620697.

How to get there: The inn is in the village of Wentbridge on the A1 3½ miles south of junction 33 on the M62.

Parking: Park in the extensive inn car park.

Length of the walk: 5½ miles. OS Map Landranger series 111 (inn GR 488172).

A paradoxical sally into the delightful valley of the Went whose image is sullied by the A1 . . . but the roar of the traffic melts away . . . wood anemones, linnets, and the sleepy village of Kirk Smeaton.

The Walk

Turn right from the inn downhill to the Went Bridge, noticing the parapet plaque to one of the aforementioned outlaws. Robin Hood and his rogues are said to have purloined many a purse at this very spot. Retreat for 30 yards and opposite Wentbridge Lane, turn left on a marked footpath. Continue on a well defined route under the A1 viaduct, following the river Went downstream. Enter Brockadale nature reserve (rare ferns) and walk on, leaving the wood near overhead power lines. Cross the meadow and turn left towards a white barred bridge. Cross, and veer left uphill to a ridge. Proceed into Little Smeaton.

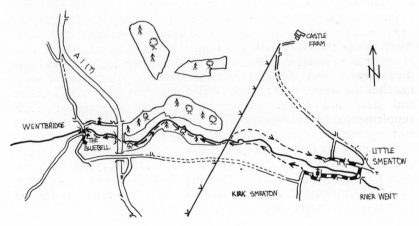

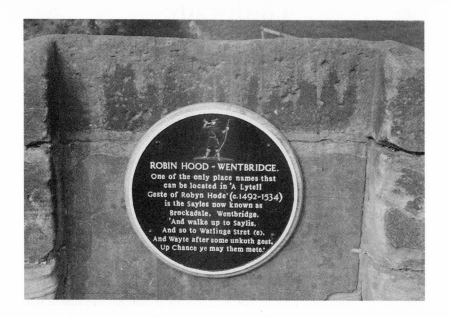

ROBIN HOOD - WENTBRIDGE.
One of the only place names that can be located in 'A Lytell Geste of Robyn Hode' (c.1492-1534) is the Sayles now known as Brockadale. Wentbridge.
'And walke up to Saylis,
And so to Watlinge Stret (e),
And Wayte after some unkuth gest,
Up Chance ye may them mete.'

Turn sharp right downhill to a bridge. Cross, and walk uphill on Hodge Lane, passing St. Peter's church (Norman chancel). Go right, round the bend and follow the twisting road past the Shoulder of Mutton inn to the next bend. Turn right on the marked footpath to Wentbridge, following the river upstream to the previously encountered power lines. At this point, you have a choice. You can either retrace your steps back into Wentbridge (when there are flowers they are well worth a second look) or alternatively you may cross the white barred bridge and go left uphill through Forestry Commission plantations. But I would caution against the latter especially if you have young children or less agile walkers in your party. The alternative route leads to a surface crossing of the busy A1 which should be negotiated with extreme care.

Other local attractions: Womersley Craft Centre.

54

Linthwaite
The Sair Inn

The combination of steep hills and some of the strongest brews ever allowed for public consumption without an aviation fuel licence, make a visit to the Sair an inevitably soporific experience.

An eccentric, thoroughly individual brewhouse pub, with a crow's nest view of the Colne Valley, the Sair (one former owner brewed sour beer and the name stuck) has no claims to decorous charm, but its 1960s vintage seating, its stone floors, coal fires and collections of old bottles create the perfect ambience for the serious sampling of hand-pulled ales. A shrine on the Campaign for Real Ale pilgrimage trail, a grotto for the ale connoisseur, the Sair serves a heady mixture of home brews including the immensely potent Enoch's Hammer (a bitter with an original gravity of 1080 – ordinary bitter weighs in at a mere 1038), Leadboiler, Old Eli and Xmas Ale. Lager drinkers can sample the equally individualistic Hoyleingerbrau. Causeway Sider (sic) is also available. Children are welcome. The dedicated master brewer of the Sair devotes all his time to producing and serving his quality ales and food is not available – bring sandwiches and an alarm clock.

The inn is not open at lunchtimes except on Saturdays and Sundays 12 noon to 3 pm. Evening hours are 7 pm to 11 pm.

Telephone: 01484 842370.

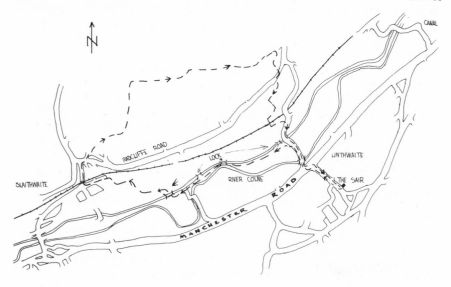

How to get there: The inn is in Linthwaite, off the Manchester Road on Hoyle Ing (runs steeply away from the river – look out for the direction sign to the pub, fixed to a wall on the left as you approach from Huddersfield).

Parking: No formal parking at the pub. Space for 4 or 5 vehicles on the road frontage only. Alternative parking on-street, but the road is steep.

Length of the walk: 3½ miles. OS Map Landranger series 110 (inn GR 100143).

Treading clog worn cobbles, you can imagine the daily grind of the old mill workers. A pleasant canalside amble is the respite between giddy heights.

The Walk

Drop down from the pub towards Manchester Road. Cross, turn left for 10 yards, and take the steps on your right, finishing the descent into the valley bottom. Go right, crossing the river Colne on a bridge, and walk on to the canal. Go left along the canal bank.

After passing the footbridge, turn right using the lock top and steer left, heading for the viaduct. Go left along the road and opposite a

56

factory entrance, turn right on London Road. Go left and first right under the viaduct, continuing round the bend past the Swan public house. Turn right along Radcliffe Road and go left on New North Road.

At the next bend, go left, following the waymarked footpath to 'Westwood Edge'. Notice the simple craftsmanship of the enduring cobbled way. On a steeply ascending track, swing right and then keep wallside left, walking on uphill to a group of houses. Go through a side gate (by the brown gate), swing left and then right to the road and turn right opposite the postbox along a quiet lane. Walk on for 300 yards and take the righthand fork along a marked footpath.

Pass in front of several cottages and swing left, going right on a waymarked path adjacent to a garage. Follow a wall down to the left and go through a kissing gate, steering diagonally right to the next gate (rusted post). Walk on, keeping wallside and squeeze through a gap by the next gate, continuing on a track between dry-stone walls. Arc right by a house, and go left over a makeshift stile opposite a ramshackle garage (turning easily missed). Cross the field, going diagonally right to a gate in the corner and turn left on the road.

Cross, turn right, and opposite the Radcliffe Road sign, fork left on a road leading to a number of cottages. Go left by the end cottage on a narrow, overgrown footpath between dry-stone walls, cross the field to the right and cross a stile, dropping down to a flight of steps under the railway. Go left under the tunnel and swing left to more steps and the road. Turn right, recrossing the river, go left up the steps, and turn left along Manchester Road. Turn right up Hoyle Ing to the pub.

Other local attractions: Marsden Moor along the A62 to the west (National Trust moorland of over 5000 acres – evidence of old Roman Road, turnpikes and remains of canal and railway tunnel workings).

Ilkley
The Midland

Built in 1864 as a railway hotel, the Midland still evokes some of the nostalgia of the footplate. Comfortably furnished with elegantly tiled twin bars, the inn is a popular rendezvous for lunchtime shoppers and workers, a collection of railway photographs and old station signs adding steamy savour to a choice of dishes which includes home-made steak pie, giant Yorkshire puddings, ham in cider, leek and potato bake and selections of toasted sandwiches and salads. Traditional roasts are available on Sundays. Children are welcome for meals.

The house ales are John Smith's and Courage Directors bitters and John Smith's Magnet. Beamish Stout, Foster's and Miller lagers, and Dry Blackthorn cider are the alternative brews.

Opening times are from Monday to Saturday 11 am to 11 pm. Sunday hours are from 12 noon to 3 pm and 7 pm to 10.30 pm.

Telephone: 01943 607433.

How to get there: The inn is on Station Road opposite the still active railway station in Ilkley.

58

Parking: Park in the inn car park to the rear . . . but why not take the rare opportunity of leaving the vehicle at home? Come by train – the platform is just a stride across the road.

Length of the walk: 4½ miles. OS Map Landranger series 104 (inn GR 118476).

A changing scenes walk circling the fashionable resort of Ilkley – riverside promenade, shady glen and wild 'Ilkla Moor baht'at'!

The Walk

Turn left from the inn and turn right down Brook Street towards the traffic lights. Cross the junction and walk on to the river, turning left by the bridge into the park. Continue to the next bridge, climb several steps and go left to find a signpost inspiration 'Dales Way Bowness 73 miles' . . . but we have not time today.

Turn right following the signposted route, keeping straight on to the left of a sports field. Swing right towards the Ilkley Lawn Tennis clubhouse and steer left opposite the entrance to find a kissing gate. Go through left and walk on along a well defined footpath through a series of kissing gates to rejoin the river bank. Cross the footbridge opposite the golf course and mount several steps. Turn left to a gate, recross the stream and go left away from the river towards the busy A65. Cross with care.

Go left for 100 yards and turn right. (The public right of way is signposted at this point but on the ground it is indeterminate.) At a 20° tangent away from the road, walk on for 50 yards only and then steer diagonally left across the next field to the corner. Cross a trickle of a stream and go right, through a gap between two upright stone pillars. Keep to the fence line for 50 yards and turn left between two further standing stones, veering away diagonally right for 200 yards across a field to intersect with a concreted farm access track (parallel lines). Go right towards a gate. Go through and continue to the next gate. Proceed forward, squeezing through a gap in a wall and going on (several hawthorn trees to your left) to find an overgrown stile. Cross and turn left uphill, walking on to Netherwood House. Swing right past a pond and the front of the house, and go left through the farmyard to Ramsgill Cottage. Go left over the gravelled drive, mount a stile and walk uphill over a grassy meadow. (On the skyline immediately in front is a group of archaeologically important rocks.)

Ascend to a plateau to the left of Hardwick House Farm and go left on the signposted path through a gap in the wall, heading towards the bottom end of woodland. Continue descending left, finding several

59

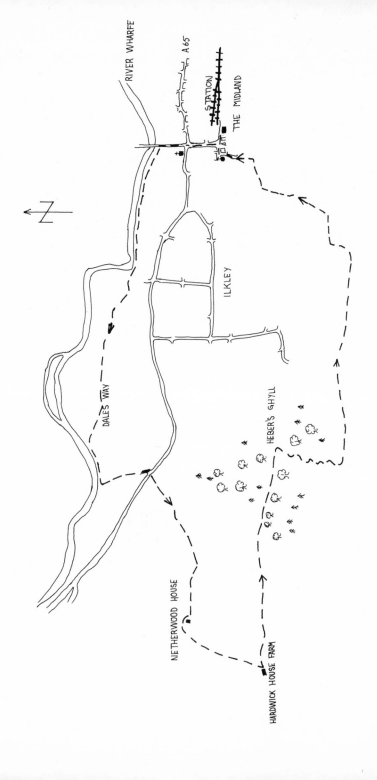

more wall stiles, aiming for distant cottages. Near the cottages, take the wall stile by the upper gate, walk on with the cottages to your left and mount a stile, continuing along the road into a broad avenue through woodland. At the bridge, go sharp right into the enchanting bower of Heber's Ghyll. The ¼ mile zig-zagging ascent which follows is demanding but exhilarating. At the summit, go left onto the edge of the moor.

Walk on, following the well worn path for about ¾ mile. Fifty yards after the house with the square tower – Overdale – turn left through a kissing gate to Westwood Drive. Turn right and keep straight on to arrive at a cattle grid. Turn left in front of the Glenmore Centre, go through another kissing gate and walk on to the next road. Cross, turn right and cut off the corner by going left down some steps. Cross the road, and take the footpath immediately in front. Turn right down Albany Walk, go left along Riddings Road and turn right back to the inn.

Other local attractions: Fashionable cafes and shops in Ilkley town centre, boating on the river and the Elizabethan Manor House Museum (includes Roman artefacts – Ilkley was once the imperial settlement of Olicana).

Cragg Vale
The Hinchliffe Arms

A retreat for Victorian mill workers, the Hinchliffe Arms can be found in the deeply cleft valley of the Cragg Brook near Hebden Bridge. Elegantly porticoed with a comfortable bar, a separate dining room and an upstairs function/children's room, the inn has a gritty individuality and intriguing associations with the Cragg Vale coiners, a notorious gang of counterfeiters who operated from the area in the 1760s.

Well known for its carvery and for its range of steak dishes, the inn offers a wide choice of home-cooked bar and restaurant meals. Prominent among the regular blackboard specials are mussels provençale, leek and Gruyère pithiviers, chicken, ham and mushroom pie, gougons of chicken and peppered entrecôte. Standard fare includes luxury chicken Kiev, beef lasagne and crusty bread, large Yorkshire puddings with a selection of toppings and variously filled French bread sandwiches. Children's portions are available. Bitter beer buffs will applaud the choice of Timothy Taylor's and Theakston's real ales. Holsten and Carlsberg lagers, draught Guinness and Strongbow cider are also on tap.

A small seating area is available at the side of the inn which is open in the summer months from 12 noon to 2 pm and 6 pm to 11 pm Monday to Saturday. Sunday hours are from 12 noon to 3 pm and 7 pm to 10.30 pm (Check opening times in winter).
Telephone: 01422 883256.

How to get there: The inn is in the hamlet of Cragg near Mytholmroyd. Access for the larger types of vehicle can be difficult: the narrow width and steepness of the short descent from the B6138 dictates care.

Parking: Park in the inn car park.

Length of the walk: 4½ miles. OS Map Landranger series 103/4 (inn GR 999233).

An energetic hike (stout footwear essential) over peat moors to Stoodley Pike ... incredible views!

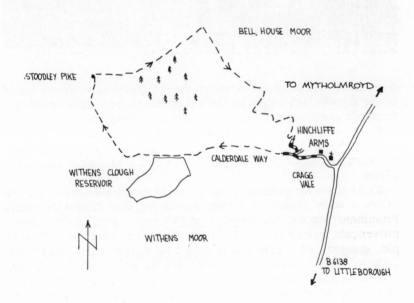

The Walk

Turn right from the inn along the road waymarked 'Calderdale Way'. Pass the Hinchliffe Hall gatehouse and steadily climb to Withens Clough Reservoir. Passing a big house on your right continue for 300 yards, heading away from the reservoir along a track signposted 'Stoodley Pike'. Make your way north-west over peat hags, aiming for the prominent obelisk erected in 1856 to commemorate the Napoleonic Wars.

From the obelisk, turn east and follow the path downhill, towards the corner of a conifer plantation. Cross a stile, and continue wallside to meet a broad walled trackway to the left. Turn left for ½ mile to a tumbledown cottage and turn right along a trackway. Go over a second stile and swing left downhill past a farmhouse, swinging right to a third stile. Cross and walk on for a short distance to a junction to your left. Turn left. Before reaching the next farmstead, go through a gate to your right and descend to a track above a linear wood. Turn left towards the farmyard and go through two gates, swinging sharp right downhill. Turn left and next right on a steep descent to the gatehouse. Turn left back to the inn.

Other local attractions: Cragg Vale church.

Boston Spa
The Admiral Hawke

The 'gallant and swift winged' victor of Quiberon Bay is admirably recalled in this roadside inn and its splendid sign. A handsome listed building in Boston Spa's fashionable High Street, the Admiral Hawke is a Samuel Smith's house, recently refurbished in traditional style.

Famous fixtures of the lounge are an oaken bar and a locally caught, glass-cased pike, a knowledgeable fellow who casts predatory eyes at the home-made food which includes a popular 'late breakfast'. Early risers can choose from wholesome Yorkshire dishes such as meat and potato pie, beef or lamb casserole, mince and onion, gammon steak or Yorkshire pudding. Salads and toasted snacks are also available. Children are welcome for meals. The inn has a well equipped games room and rear yard patio tables for the summer months. The liquid fare is Samuel Smith's Bitter and Mild, Ayingerbrau and Diet Pils lagers and Cider Reserve.

Opening times are from Monday to Saturday 11.30 am to 3 pm and 6 pm to 11 pm. Sunday hours are from 12 noon to 3 pm and 7 pm to 10.30 pm.

Telephone: 01937 842170.

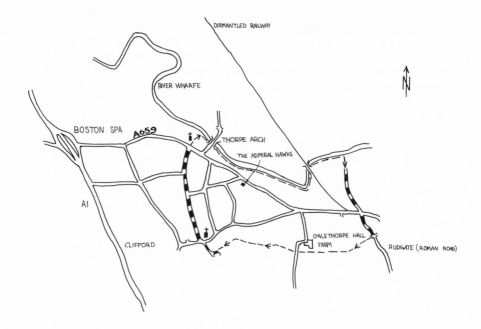

How to get there: The inn is on High Street in the riverside village of Boston Spa near the A1 south-east of Wetherby.

Parking: Park in the car park to the rear of the inn.

Length of the walk: 6½ miles. OS Map Landranger series 105 (inn GR 437452).

The longest walk in this collection, but a gentle ramble nonetheless, through fields and water meadows.

The Walk

Turn left from the inn along High Street passing the elegant Georgian mansions whose provenance springs from the discovery of a local spa in 1744. Continue, to find a footpath (Holgate Lane) between the Central Garage and St. Mary's church. Turn right to the river. Before turning right along the banks of the Wharfe, walk to your left, noting the fragmentary remains of a salmon keeper's cottage hard by the weir. Turn right and walk on under the bridge uphill to the site of the Spa Baths (now fashionable bungalows). In comparatively recent times the medicinal waters – good for 'general relaxation, bilious disorders,

66

glandular obstructions, and scirrhosities, stomach complaints, and spontaneous vomitings' – could be had for threepence per glass.

Proceed bankside for about 1 mile to a pronounced bend in the river and cross a stile uphill, walking alongside the perimeter fence of a paper mill. Drop down, cross a second stile and walk under an abandoned railway bridge into a broad meadow. Follow the stream down for ¼ mile and turn right just beyond the river island, along a track (The Ebor Way) to the A659. Cross the road, and walk on along the Roman road (Rudgate), passing The Paddocks and Rudgate Cottage. Turn right along the St. Helens Farm access. Keep straight on, walking without deviation between the farm and outbuildings, passing ponds to your left and then to your right. Turn right towards a barn and go left fieldside to a stile over an electric fence. Cross, and walk on keeping to the edge of a field and go left along a hedge and then right until you come to a stile. Cross and turn right for 20 yards only and go left. At the intersection of the next track, turn left for a short distance and turn right onto a footpath under power lines aiming for the distant steeple of St. Edward's church.

Swing left along a fence line and drop down to a road in the village of Clifford. Turn right along Old Mill Lane and walk on to a T junction. Turn left along the front of the church and turn right along Chapel Lane. Continue on Boston Road and Church Street into Boston Spa. Turn right along High Street back to the inn.

Other local attractions: Bramham Park (stately home and horse trials) and the tiny, little-known village of Newton Kyme, 2 miles to the east (13th/14th century church of St. Andrew, Newton Hall and the remains of a 10½ acre Roman fort, part of whose stone rampart is still visible).

Holme
The Fleece

Holme is where the heart is and big heartedness is a feature of the hilltop Fleece. In West Yorkshire's outback, the Fleece began life as a livery stable, serving pack horse routes across the Pennines. Oats and water have today given way to steak and fine ales, garnished with an infectious brand of Yorkshire humour regularly harnessed in the cause of good works. In its homely, welcoming bar, bright with all manner of plaques and trophies, the Fleece sells maps and walking sticks in aid of the Moorland Rescue Team. It is also dedicated to helping the Royal National Lifeboat Institution whose craft 'The Fleece Holme Boat' is based at Filey.

Food at the Fleece is from the ethnic mould. Try the daily special – typically mince pie, meat and potato pie or fresh haddock – or choose a standard offering such as mixed grill, roast chicken with apple sauce and stuffing, Cumberland sausage or trout. And will the Falstaffian landlord persuade you to try one of his liqueured ice cream delights? Definitely not for motorists! The inn also serves a traditional Sunday roast lunch. Children are welcome for meals. A wide range of beverages is available at The Fleece – tea and coffee (served outside normal licensing hours if required), hand-pulled Theakston Bitter, Mild and Old Peculier, Younger Bitter and IPA, McEwan, Harp and Becks lagers, Dry Blackthorn and Autumn Gold ciders, draught Guinness and draught fresh orange juice. Walkers are particularly welcome (plastic bootees are provided!). The inn has seasonal hanging baskets and a pleasant seating area to the front.

Opening times are Monday to Friday 11 am to 3 pm and 7pm to 11 pm. Saturday hours are 11 am to 3 pm and 5 pm to 11 pm. On Sunday, the inn is open from 11 am to 10.30 pm.

Telephone: 01484 683449.

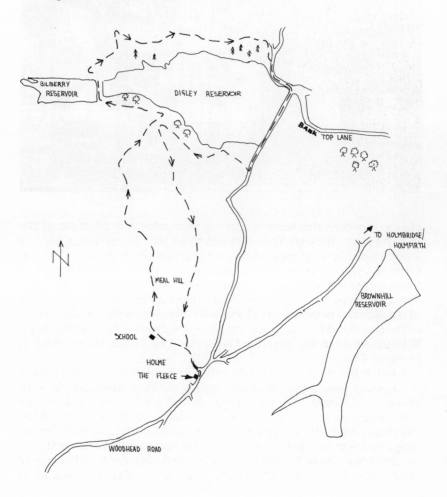

How to get there: The inn is south-west of Holmfirth on the Woodhead Road near the Yorkshire/Lancashire boundary.

Parking: Park in the car park to the rear.

Length of the walk: 3 miles. OS Map Landranger series 110 (inn GR 108060).

An easy and popular orbit of Digley Reservoir.

The Walk

Turn left from the inn and turn left again up a cobbled (at first) lane, rising uphill, past the school and Meal Hill to a fork in the track. Go right, downhill to the shores of Digley Reservoir and go left on the well-trodden footpath on a clockwise circuit of the banks.

Cross the dam wall and turn right over a parking area. Go left through a kissing gate and continue bankside to a stream. Turn left, following a signposted footpath, gradually veering right, away from the reservoir over several stiles to Holme. Turn left opposite The Nook, and turn right back to the inn.

Linton
The Windmill

A relaxing ancient and modern inn offering a conservatory and three cosy cornered bars timelessly dressed in brasses, prints and fresh flowers, the Windmill is developing a deserved reputation for good food and fine ales. Watchwords of the kitchen – freshness, home cooked and presentation – are self evident in a versatile menu which typically features gougons of monkfish, poached salmon, chicken in lemon sauce, steak and ale pie and cashew nut stroganoff. Children are welcome for meals and, for lazy days, the inn has an attractive beer garden to the rear.

The house ales are hand-pulled Theakston Bitter, XB and Younger Scotch Bitter, together with McEwan and Becks lagers, Dry Blackthorn cider and draught Guinness.

Opening times are Monday to Saturday 11.30 to 3 pm and 5.30 pm to 11 pm. Sunday hours are 12 noon to 3 pm and 7 pm to 10.30 pm. Telephone: 01937 582938.

How to get there: The inn is off the A659 in the pretty village of Linton near Wetherby.

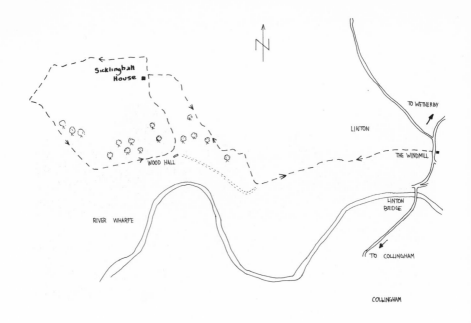

Parking: Park in the inn car park.

Length of the walk: 5 miles. OS Map Landranger series 104 (inn GR 390468).

A tree-adorned introduction to the Ebor Way with the tempting possibility of popping in for afternoon tea at the rather grand Wood Hall.

The Walk

Walk down Trip Lane opposite the inn to the entrance to Wood Hall and turn right, following the waymarked path to Sicklinghall into a wood. Leave the wood and continue along a field edge, swinging left, following a well defined weaving path along the perimeter of a second wood. Follow the waymarkers into the wood, leave it and walk on hedgeside, swinging left to a group of houses.

Turn right along the tarmac road, and opposite the Sicklinghall House sign, turn left (no marker), following the hedge without deviation to join the access road to Paddock House. Turn left to Paddock House (fascinating architecture), swing left and right and left

again, drinking in the view of Wharfedale. At the sharp bend (the road leads on to Carlstonhill Farm) go left along the marked footpath towards Wood Hall. (Just before you reach the buildings, a track darts off right to greet the Wharfe – an excellent detour if you have time before that treat you promised yourself.)

Go through a gate and keep straight on, passing new houses and a chapel. Swing left by the back of the hall and ready your civvy footwear for your appointment with the spout. Either take the grand exit along the drive, or go left and follow the marked bridleway through woodland and up a short hill to Sicklinghall House. Turn right again and retrace your steps to Trip Lane. Turn left back to the inn.

Other local attractions: The nearby market town of Wetherby.

Ackworth
The Rustic Arms

In splendid isolation betwixt twin villages, the Rustic Arms is one of West Yorkshire's newest inns. A vision of tradition? Honeysuckle by the porch and hearth brasses? Forget it. This inn is to the licensed trade what the Pompidou Centre is to Paris! Originally a drab smallholding, transformed into a plush multi-windowed hacienda with extensive facilities for children, the inn offers beleaguered parents the ultimate respite. Inside is a large family room equipped with pool tables, game machines and kiddies' rides – but outside, out of earshot, youngsters can cast a line, canoe on the barside lake, go-cart on the specially constructed track, or take the challenge of the adventure playground . . . and they have their own special menu.

Adults are equally well catered for in the immensely spacious lounges which provide both light snacks and restaurant meals. Standard fare, served in the bar or on the patio, includes omelettes, chilli-con-carne, steak and gammon sandwiches, giant Yorkshire puddings and vegetable lasagne, supplemented by daily specials such as chicken Kiev stuffed with lobster and prawns. For parents spared bailing duty, the extensive restaurant menu lists duckling a l'orange,

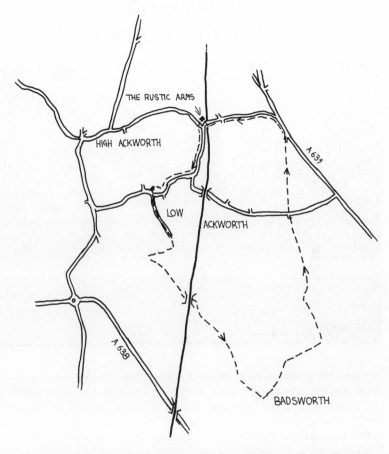

pork marsala, plaice Dieppe (filled with prawns and mushrooms in a white wine sauce) a range of sauced steaks and mixed grill. The liquid cheer is John Smith's and Stones bitters, Black Label, Miller and Foster's lagers, Dry Blackthorn and Woodpecker ciders and draught Guinness.

The inn is open from Monday to Saturday 11.30 am to 3 pm and 7 pm (5 pm in summer) to 11 pm. Sunday hours are from 12 noon to 3 pm and 7 pm to 10.30 pm.

Telephone: 01977 794136.

How to get there: The inn is on a minor road between High Ackworth and East Hardwick, south-east of Wakefield.

Parking: Park in the inn car park.

Length of the walk: 4½ miles. OS Map Landranger series 111 (inn GR 181454).

A country stroll by paths and quiet byways. If time permits examine some of the district's interesting architecture which includes Ackworth school erected in 1758 and St. Mary's church, Badsworth.

The Walk

Turn left from the rear of the inn and turn right along Station Road (a roadside nature reserve) into Low Ackworth. Continue round the bend past Ackworth Howards School and turn left down Tan House Lane. At the point where a ditch to your right meets the river Went, turn right over a stile, following a path upstream. Turn left over a bridge and cross a field diagonally left. Cross a second stile and head for a barn and an underpass in a railway embankment beyond. Turn left under the railway and swing right on a farm track, following a well defined route into Badsworth. Walking uphill, turn left along Grove Lane, dropping down past a farmhouse and swinging right to a bridleway sign. Turn left to re-cross the Went near a sewage works and walk on to the road. Cross and walk uphill to the A639. Turn left. After 200 yards, turn left again along Station Road (little traffic) and continue to the inn.

Other local attractions: Nostell Priory (18th century National Trust property housing a rare collection of Chippendale furniture) and Top Farm, West Hardwick (agricultural museum).

Widdop
The Pack Horse

At an elevation of 978 ft, the lonely Pack Horse inn is a whitewashed beacon. Visible for miles around, it once served the gruelling pack horse trade. Today it caters for hardy visitors to the wind slammed moors. Rugged, yet wonderfully relaxing with long distance views, the inn has twin bars, frequently log-flamed, proudly displaying a Klondyke collection of photographs recording the achievements of Victorian reservoir pioneers.

For a wilderness once dubbed 'Dawson City', Widdop is surprisingly well served, the inn providing a wide and sophisticated range of bar meals, hallmarked by home-made soups and blackboard specials such as jambalaya (hot spicy pork with fresh ginger and peppers), leek and potato bake topped with cheese and almonds, pancakes stuffed with chicken and mushrooms, steak au poivre with brandy and cream, fresh strawberry and lychee pavlova and hot mincemeat torte. Fresh local pheasant and grouse are available in season. The standard menu lists crevettes, cheese and onion pie, fillet steak, cottage hotpot and open sandwiches. Children and parties (advance notice requested) are welcome for meals.

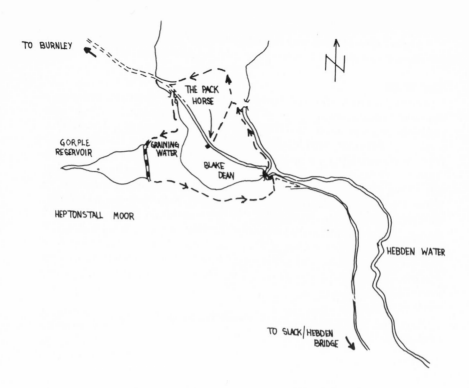

A free house, the Pack Horse offers a stallion string of ales – Thwaites, Younger, IPA, Theakston XB and Ruddles hand-pulled bitters, together with Carlsberg lager and Woodpecker and Strongbow ciders.

The inn is not open at lunchtimes October to April (except on Saturdays and Sundays – 12 noon to 2 pm and 12 noon to 2.30 pm respectively – evening hours 7 pm to 11 pm and 10.30 pm respectively). The rest of the year, opening times Monday to Sunday are 12 noon to 3 pm and 7 pm to 11 pm (10.30 pm on Sunday).

Telephone: 01422 842803.

How to get there: The inn is on the moorland road between Hebden Bridge and Colne.

Parking: Park in the inn car park.

Length of the walk: 4 miles. OS Map Landranger series 103 (inn GR 952317).

78

A bog-trot apprenticeship with impressive views for aspiring Penninewayers. You will discover that they built reservoirs up here for good reason.

The Walk

Opposite the inn, take the signposted track over pasture, crossing a stile and heading for the edge of a plantation. Cross a second stile, and turn left on a metalled road (the Pennine Way), dropping downhill to a gate. Go through, turn left for a short distance on the Hebden-Colne road and go right to a stile, following the permissive bridleway to 'Lower Gorple and Colden'. Proceed uphill and swing right, turning left along Gorple's dam-top causeway. Turn left along the road to Blake Dean and walk on for about a mile. Turn left on a footpath downhill towards the roadbridge. At the road, turn left and cross the bridge, going immediately right into Walshaw Dean. Swing left uphill with the impressive Hebden Water at your elbow, continuing to a point opposite a barn and a double arched bridge. Turn left, following a marked footpath. Veer left by a fence line and continue back to the inn.

Other local attractions: Hardcastle Crags (National Trust) and the hilltop village of Heptonstall.

Shadwell
The Red Lion

A crimsoned escapee from Trafalgar Square guards this popular watering hole in Shadwell near Leeds. A one time combined beerhouse and blacksmith's, this ideal walkers' inn enjoys a lively trade, heightened by a reputation for fine ale.

Twin bars graced with jugs, pots, and rustic prints offer wholesome home-cooked meals. The standard fare features steak pie, roast beef and Yorkshire pudding, braised sausages, chilli-con-carne, chicken curry and double decker sandwiches, supplemented by daily specials such as cod in parsley sauce, meat and potato pie, chicken casserole and cumberland pie. A hallowed meal in itself, the excellent hand-pulled Tetley Bitter is joined by hand-pulled Tetley Mild and Burton Bitter, Castlemaine and Carlsberg lagers, Olde English cider, Guinness and draught white wine. Children are welcome for meals. The inn has an outside patio area for summer dining.

The Red Lion is open from Monday to Saturday – 11.30 am to 11 pm. Sunday hours are 12 noon to 3 pm and 7 pm to 10.30 pm. Telephone: 0113 273 7463.

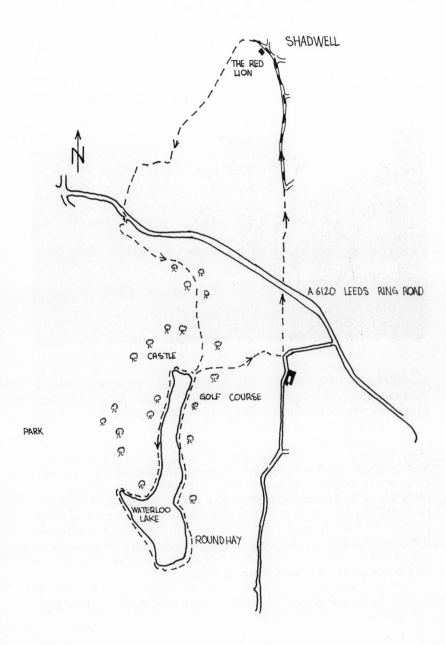

SHADWELL

THE RED
LION

A 6120 LEEDS RING ROAD

CASTLE

GOLF COURSE

PARK

WATERLOO
LAKE

ROUNDHAY

How to get there: The inn is in the village of Shadwell north of Leeds.

Parking: Park in the extensive inn car park.

Length of the walk: 3¾ miles. OS Map Landranger series 104 (inn GR 340398).

A saunter to one of the best municipal parks in England. Bluebell woods, a mock castle, and a splendid fishing lake (seen to best advantage over coffee and cream horns in the water's edge cafe) add to the delights.

The Walk

Turn left from the inn along Main Street and turn left again, following a signposted and well defined footpath to the Leeds ring road. Cross, and take a signposted track, dropping down and turning right over a hump-backed bridge. Mount a stile and go left following the serpentine course of a stream through woodland to a second bridge. Turn right over the bridge, noticing a castellated folly on the hillside. (The Nicholson family who bequeathed their Roundhay home to the city were involved in a number of job creation schemes – the castle and Waterloo Lake to your left involved a cast of thousands.) Proceeding right, walk along the lakeside to the cafe (a mid-walk break is permitted).

Continue the circuit. (Below the new dam wall is a site as infamous as Changi prison. Few of my generation survived Arctic plunges in Roundhay Open Air Swimming Pool without skin grafts.) At the lake's top end, go right uphill into woodland and veer left, crossing a narrow fairway of Cobble Hall Golf Club. Turn right and steer left to the intersection of the club driveway and a footpath from the left. Turn left along the footpath to the Leeds ring road. Cross and continue without deviation, following a marked bridleway to merge with Colliers Lane. Walk on to Main Street and turn left to the inn.

Other local attractions: Shadwell Cricket Club.

Farnley Tyas
The Golden Cock

The ale-house origins of this 400 year old listed building are consigned to ancient history. With jet set panache, gourmet food and vintage wines, this thoroughly modern inn is a gilded bird indeed. A marbled cocktail bar decorated in Italian art deco style and an intimate restaurant set the scene for fashionable dining, the modern English cuisine attracting customers from both sides of the Pennines. The hallmarks of freshness, culinary flair and attention to detail shine through in an appetising menu, the description 'home-made' extending to breads, pastas and gateaux.

Alongside their bin end bargains, to the occasional strains of a jazz band, you can enjoy daily blackboard specials such as veal escalope with onions, game pie, braised oxtail in red wine, fillet of pork in paprika sauce, red bream, king prawns and Aberdeen haddock, whilst more formal diners can select from an extensive list. This includes salmon, sole and spinach roulade with a watercress sauce, fillet of beef with a Stilton souffle, parfait of ducks' livers studded with pistachio nuts and served with toasted brioche, dark chocolate torte flavoured with framboise in a white chocolate and raspberry sauce and apricot

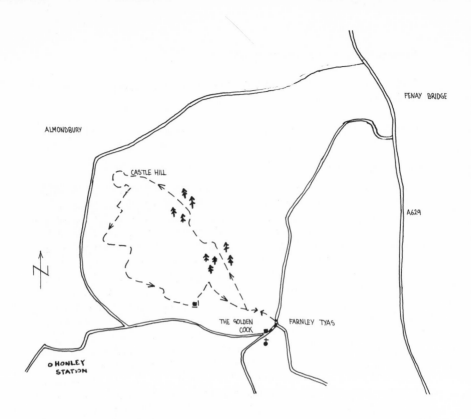

and almond pastry puffs. The inn has an upstairs dining room, the venue for Sunday carvery lunches which are especially popular with families. Despite its sophistication, the inn welcomes walkers. The small, traditionally furnished pub bar, sandwiched between its more glamorous room mates, is the place for map reading. The inn also has an outside seating area.

The Golden Cock offers a wide variety of classical wines but beer drinkers are not forgotten. Hand-pulled Tetley and Burton bitters are available, together with a guest beer, and Castlemaine and Lowenbrau lagers, Guinness and Gaymer's Olde English cider are also on tap.

Opening times are from 11.30 am to 3 pm and 6 pm to 11 pm Monday to Saturday. Sunday hours are 12 noon to 3 pm and 7 pm to 10.30 pm.

Telephone: 01484 666644.

How to get there: The inn is in the village of Farnley Tyas south of Huddersfield.

84

Parking: Park in the inn car park.

Length of the walk: 5 miles. OS Map Landranger series 110 (inn GR 165128).

Come in Spring for a blooming woodland spectacular. And climb (plenty of puff needed) to the 900 ft tower on Castle Hill – giddy views.

The Walk

Objective, Castle Hill – it stands out like a giant's thumb on the dizzy skyline to the north. Turn left from the inn along the road for 30 yards, and turn left again, following a signposted footpath downhill. Bear left and where the path bifurcates swing right wallside, continuing your descent into woodland. Walk on, leave the wood and cross a narrow field end, re-entering the wood and continuing to a stream. Cross and climb uphill to a lane. Turn right for 200 yards and follow the signposted path on the left, walking up and bearing left to a track. Go 5 yards left, and follow a rising footpath (signpost missing) towards the tower, built in 1897 to celebrate the reign of Queen Victoria. Turn right at the road and make a circuit of Castle Hill.

Drop down to the road, turn right and go left, looking out for a footpath (sign missing) next to a whitewashed farmhouse to your right. Turn right and walk on to a farmstead. Just before reaching the buildings, turn left along a track bounded by dry-stone walls. At the next field, go left, right, and right again by the edge of a coppice, and walk on for about 150 yards from the edge of the trees to a gap in the wall to your left. Go left following the yellow arrow marker, steering 45° left across the meadow. Turn right at the field boundary and follow a barbed wire fence for 150 yards to a gate. Turn left, crossing a stile and walking on down the middle of a field towards cottages.

Turn left up the access track, turn right in front of and left by the side of Long Meadow and go through a gap in the wall. Veer right across the corner of the meadow and go through a gap in the wall, turning left to the field corner. Cross a stile and swing right. Cross another stile and cut across the middle of a field, walking in the direction of the church steeple. Cross five more stiles and fields, keeping to the bottoms, and go through a gap by the gate to join the path used on the outward journey. Keep straight on, turn right uphill to the road and turn right back to the inn.

Other local attractions: Golcar Museum (west of Huddersfield) – restored weavers' cottages and demonstrations.

Emley
The White Horse

Poised for action like a lifeboat on its slip, this hillside inn has only recently reverted to its age old name. And there hangs a tale. To the dismay of villagers, it was dubbed the Emley Village Inn by an entrepreneurial former owner. A new landlord and a referendum later and it's hi-ho Silver and away!

Long and low beamed, the inn has a tap-room, a comfortable Delph-racked lounge and an intimate restaurant hung with pictures by a local artist. With the accent on home cooking using fresh ingredients, the menu offers a selection of bar and restaurant meals which vary with the seasons. Special recipe soups, steaks, beef in Guinness pie, cheesy shepherd's pie, pork stroganoff, grilled trout, salads, a range of vegetarian dishes and various fruit pies, crumbles and compotes are all winning friends. A traditional roast is served on Sundays. Children are welcome for meals and discounted fare for pensioners is offered Monday to Saturday. The house bitter is Tetley. Carlsberg and Castlemaine lagers, Olde English cider and draught Guinness are also available.

The inn is open from Monday to Saturday 11.30 am to 3 pm and 6 pm to 11 pm. Sunday hours are 12 noon to 3 pm and 7 pm to 10.30 pm.
Telephone: 01924 374942.

How to get there: The inn is in the village of Emley (the one sprouting the tallest footpath marker in the world), off the A636 to the south-west of Wakefield.

Parking: Park in the inn car park.

Length of the walk: 4 miles. OS Map Landranger series 110 (inn GR 243131).

Enjoy this ramble through quiet pastures. Emley's famous TV mast will guide your way.

The Walk

Turn left from the inn towards the village centre, and turn left again down Church Street. Walk on to the Green Dragon pub and go left by the side of the church, following the waymarked track past the churchyard. At the end of a wall, swing right and cross a meadow to a footbridge and a stile. Cross, swing left and then right by the field

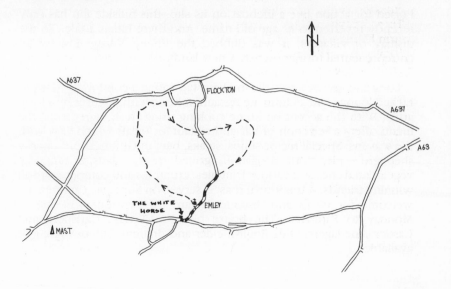

corner and cross the next field on a well trodden footpath, going right in the field corner and left, following the hedge line on a slight incline towards the farm. Where the hedge ends and the wall begins, turn right through a gap and swing left towards the farm.

Go over a stile by the gate and turn right for 80 yards only. Follow the footpath sign to the left, going diagonally right, aiming for the marker post 40 yards to the right of the gate. Go left across the footbridge and go left again at the field corner stile, turning right to the next stile. Cross, go right and left by the field edges, dropping downhill to a stile. Cross, continuing along a broad track to a stile and an access road. Cross, and turn right passing several cottages. Ignore the left hand road and proceed round the bend uphill, walking on to the last house. About 20 yards past this building, look out on your right for an unmarked, narrow and overgrown track between two walls. Turn right, heading towards a wood. Go left over a stile into the wood, walking uphill to a stile. Cross and continue over a meadow to the next stile. Cross and walk on to the road. Turn right for a short distance uphill. Opposite the newly built houses, turn left along the farm track.

Arriving at the private access drive to the farm, go left downhill for 50 yards only and turn right over a stile following the waymarked Kirklees Way. At the next stile, go diagonally right, cutting off the corner of the field, aiming for a tall yellow topped (somewhat weathered) marker post at the edge of a copse. Go right into the copse, cross a footbridge to a stile, and go left, keeping hedge side to a gate. Turn right (waymarked), heading for a point midway between the farm buildings to your left and Emley Moor Mast to your right. About 50 yards before you come to the next gate, veer right downhill, crossing a shallow depression to the road. Turn left into Emley along Clough Road, Rectory Lane and Church Street. Turn right back to the inn.

Other local attractions: Yorkshire Sculpture Park at West Bretton (free entry) and Cannon Hall Country Park.

Baildon
The Half Way House

An attractive roadhouse on the old coach road midway between Otley and Bradford, this inn happily marries tradition with modernity. Completely refurbished in country mode with a fine display of bric-a-brac and rustic pictures, the inn has a bright and inviting interior which is conducive to relaxed eating. A popular addition to the Half Way House is the recently enlarged enclosed children's play area. This is very popular with parents in the summer, who can eat and drink and keep an eye on their young ones all at the same time.

A 'Big Steak' establishment, the inn has a carnivorous streak offering sirloins, T bones and gargantuan 32 oz rumps. The standard menu also lists steak and kidney pie, chicken Kiev, lasagne, fillet of plaice, broccoli and cream cheese pie and mushroom tagliatelle. Served in French style baguettes, roast topside of beef and honey roast ham sandwiches are particularly good value. Hedonistically tempting sweets include knickerbocker glory, toffee and butterscotch sundae and a traditional hot pudding of the day. Other daily specials typically offer grilled salmon, Yorkshire sandwich (roast beef, kidney and sausage), authentic curry and leek and Stilton bake. Children are

89

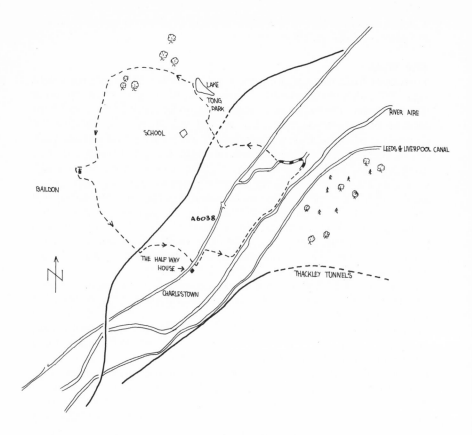

welcome for meals. A Tetley house, the inn serves Tetley Bitter, Marston's Pedigree, and Castlemaine, Carlsberg and Lowenbrau lagers, Gaymer's Olde English cider and draught Guinness.

Opening times are from Monday to Saturday 11 am to 11 pm. Sunday hours are 12 noon to 3 pm and 7 pm to 10.30 pm.

Telephone: 01274 584610.

How to get there: The inn is on the A6038 at Charlestown near Baildon.

Parking: Park in the inn car park.

Length of the walk: 3½ miles. OS Map Landranger series 104 (inn GR 164388).

A high contrasts walk – a riverbank, a dingle of a dell (see the reverse of the new £10 note) and Baildon's old ginnels.

The Walk

Turn right from the inn along the road, and after 250 yards turn right again following the marked footpath to the River Aire. Turn left along the riverbank. There is a noticeable sparsity of wildlife here and faint aromas of something not nice so we will keep on, passing the footbridge of 1889, and swinging left by a rifle range to the road. Turn left by the golf driving range. Walk on to the sharp left bend and keep going forward (no sign), with the golf greens to your right, to the road. Cross, and take the steps to the left of the bus shelter to a road. Cross, go through a gap in the wall and a kissing gate, climbing towards a church-like building (now a private house). Squeeze between the building and a row of terraced houses to the left on a narrow path and go right for 10 yards and then left onto a rough track leading to a new estate – The Paddock. Turn right to the entrance of Tong Park Centre and go left by the boundary wall.

Walk on to a gate and, using a stile, proceed left and right downhill on a track to a lake and a cricket ground rivalling anything in Pickwick Papers (the £10 note connection again). Turn left by the ground perimeter and, at the back of the scorehouse, swing left into a copse, going left again after 300 yards, leaving the wood and heading for a telegraph pole in the meadow. Turn left to the meeting of tracks at the four oak trees. Fork left, in the direction of the farm and the high ground, and climb the stile to the left of the gate. Swing left, keeping wallside uphill to the next stile. Cross, and go left at the base of a hillock. Go left again up several steps, walking between rugby and soccer pitches. Walk on to the road.

Without changing direction, walk down Hey Gate Lane (school to your right) and turn right along Hall Cliff to the church. Turn left through the churchyard, and keep left on a footpath to the next road. Cross, and continue on a ginnel to a road. Cross, turn left at the cottage, and turn right at Brook Hill using the marked ginnel, passing Brook House to the tunnel under the railway. Go under and turn left to Kirklands Lane, walking down the length of this lane to the road. Turn right back to the inn.

Other local attractions: Shipley Glen, a beauty spot accessed by a vintage cable-hauled tramway, and Saltaire, a 19th century model village built by philanthropist Sir Titus Salt.

Goose Eye
The Turkey Inn

An unassuming building in the contortionist hollow of Goose Eye near Keighley, the 200 year old Turkey inn lies opposite a redundant mill which once produced banknotes for the colonies. There is a pleasant seating area for the inn in the summer months on what was formerly the mill pond. Smart, restrained and comfortable like a Sunday best cap, the inn has grown over the years, expanding into adjacent cottages whose character smoulders on in open hearths and low beams. A former Kings house (the monogrammed stained glass windows tell the takeover tale) the Turkey is an inn of appealing odd corners. The eccentric use of old barrel staves in the bar and ceilings and the nostalgic gallery of historical prints and photographs add to the personality.

Served either in the tastefully furnished dining area or in the bar, food is freshly cooked and versatile. Steaks, headed by a gargantuan 32 oz rump, dominate, but there is a wide range of alternative dishes such as Yorkshire pudding with various fillings, steak and kidney pie, gammon, fillet of haddock and vegetarian offerings like lasagne and broccoli and cream cheese bake. Seasonally available puddings include bilberry pie and sticky toffee pudding. Children are welcome for meals. For connoisseurs of real ale, a visit to the Turkey can be a lingering affair. Brewed locally, the superb, plummily astringent Goose Eye Bitter is highly addictive. Tetley and Burton bitters, Skol, Castlemaine and Lowenbrau lagers, Gaymer's Olde English cider and Guinness are also on tap.

Opening times at the Turkey inn are from Monday to Saturday (but closed Monday lunchtime) 12 noon to 3 pm (5 pm on Saturday) and 5.30 pm (7 pm on Saturday) to 11 pm. Sunday hours are 12 noon to 3 pm and 7 pm to 10.30 pm.

Telephone: 01535 681339.

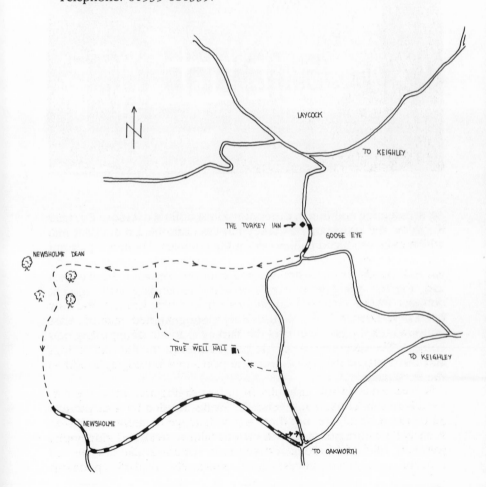

How to get there: The inn is in the hamlet of Goose Eye, 2½ miles west of Keighley, off Holme House Lane.

Parking: Park in the large car park opposite the inn.

Length of the walk: 5 miles. OS Map Landranger series 104 (inn GR 029405).

A ramble in delightful countryside, leafy, blossomed and lusciously berried with the seasons (one steep ascent).

The Walk

Turn right from the inn and follow the S bend over the bridge. Walk on for 80 yards uphill, and at the next bend turn right, following the footpath sign to the right. Cross the beck on the little bridge, bearing left upstream to a pond. Go left, and swing right by the pond, continuing upstream to a galvanised bridge. Veer right opposite the bridge, proceeding uphill and pass a cottage to your right. Take the left hand track signposted to 'Newsholme', descending and passing through a white gate to a beautiful meadow. The pack horse bridge and its ancient clapper twin are real gems. Cross the bridge, and steering left by the fenceline, continue on a well defined path uphill. The bilberries here are profuse. This is my kind of 'pick your own'! At the top, go through a gap in the wall, and follow a footpath to a cluster of dwellings at Newsholme.

At this point, like many walkers before me, I had intended to turn left on a public right of way which is clearly marked on the OS sheet. However, a local inhabitant who has lived in the hamlet all her life, told me that the path exists only in the eyes of the cartographers! But do not despair! Weave right and then left, passing the quaintly ivied church of St. John, dropping down on the road to a track opposite Green End Farm. Turn left down the track and walk on to the road. Turn left in the direction of Goose Eye, using the left hand footway, and continue to the signposted access to True Well Hall. Turn left on the access, and walk on, passing the hall and Carr Laithe, and swing right to the aforementioned galvanised footbridge. This time, cross and turn right, retracing your steps to the inn.

Other local attractions: Keighley and Worth Valley Railway in Keighley (steam trains).

The irresistible Clapper Bridge at Newsholme Dean.

Eccup
The New Inn

Contemplating his Yorkshire pint, a monocled huntsman smirks out at distant Leeds. High on the gable of the New Inn, Tetley's famous trade mark enjoys uninterrupted views over pastures and cornfields, attracting a lively trade. The New Inn has an interesting past. Originally a cottage, it became a makeshift coffee house in Victorian times, serving navvies from the nearby reservoir construction site at Eccup. In celebrating the birthday of a worker, hot drinks were elbowed in favour of stronger brews, and the modern inn was born.

Recently refurbished, its comfortable inter-linked lounges handsomely embellished with original paintings, the New Inn is today a popular country destination with its own clay pigeon shooting club. It has a particular appeal for families, providing a large children's room and an extensive beer garden generously equipped with swings, slides, climbing frames and bouncy castles in summer. Barbecue kits may be hired and grill-ready meat packs are available if booked ahead. If your wild frontier days are past, settle for a home-cooked bar meal, choosing from a standard menu which includes steak, mixed grill, a selection of hot sandwiches, fresh salads and deep fried haddock.

Alternative dishes such as steak and kidney pie (with a proper suet crust), lamb chops, Cumberland sausage, lasagne, and locally caught trout and pike are available as blackboard specials. Sunday roasts offer beef, lamb, pork and chicken. Children are catered for separately.

Even though he has only one good eye, the huntsman pulls a fine drop of hand-drawn bitter and mild, recently joined by a second real ale from the Marston stable. Castlemaine and Carlsberg lagers are also on tap, together with Gaymer's Olde English cider and Guinness.

The New Inn is open from Monday to Saturday from 11 am to 3 pm and 5.30 pm to 11 pm. Sunday hours are from 12 noon to 3 pm and 7 pm to 10.30 pm.

Telephone: 0113 288 6335.

How to get there: Worth searching for, the inn, near the hamlet of Eccup, is best approached from the A61 Leeds to Harrogate Road, turning left along Alwoodley lane and right along King Lane to Five Lane Ends.

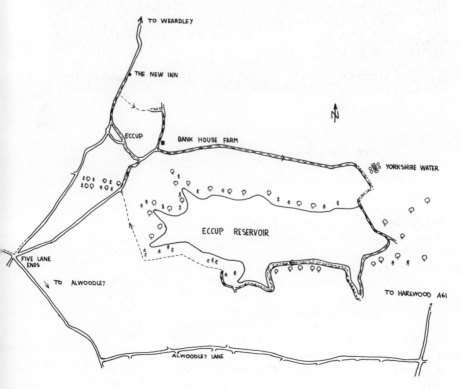

97

Parking: Park in the inn car park.

Length of the walk: 5 miles. OS Map Landranger series 104 (inn GR 289429).

A good leg-stretcher around the shores of Eccup Reservoir, a site of special scientific interest supporting a variety of wildlife where, if you are lucky, you may witness one of the most spectacular displays of mayfly courtship in the county. Anglers, quell your ardour – NO FISHING!

The Walk

Turn left from the inn and walk along the roadside verge for 200 yards. Turn left, following a signposted footpath across a field to a wall. Cross and continue forward with a hedge on your right hand to a stile and turn right along a track to Bank House Farm. Turn left along the metalled access to Eccup Water Treatment Works and walk on for ¾ mile (enjoy the music of the skylarks, lapwings and curlews). Drop down to the left and swing right to the works access, turning sharp right through a white gate, following a short footpath to the left alongside a beech hedge. Turn right once more on roadway to greet 6,410,000 cubic metres of water and bear left along the dam top to a lodge.

Turn right through a green kissing gate and weave your way for about a mile to pass through a second green kissing gate near Goodrick Lodge. Bear right and follow a track, emerging on the edge of a field. Keeping to the edge, walk on with the plantation to your right. In the field corner, turn right over a stile. Drop downhill, cross a second stile and continue forward over pasture to a third stile. Turn right onto the road (little traffic) and turn left opposite The Rookery, ascending and walking past Mount House. Turn right a short distance along the road to the inn.

Other local attractions: Golden Acre Park (gardens, wildfowl and cafe) and Harewood House (an impressive mansion open to the public).

Wainstalls
The Delvers

Displaying a front parlour collection of knick-knacks and decorative prints, this immensely comfortable inn will delight all those who remember old fashioned hospitality. In full view of the wide open moors, the inn attracts breathless walkers, cyclists, fell runners and horse riders, as well as the more sedentary sorts.

Reserved, yet lively enough to offer live jazz on Monday evenings, the inn (its name honours local quarrymen) serves a range of quality dishes such as home-made chicken soup with cream, roast ham salad and ploughman's lunch. The Sunday largesse featuring hot sausages, bread and dripping and pizza slices is excellent value for money! Children are welcomed into the conservatory which is provided with crayons and colouring books. A large grassed play area is available outside. The hand-pulled ale is from the Thwaites Brewery – Bitter and Mild. The other choices are Castlemaine and Carlsberg lagers, Woodpecker and Strongbow ciders and draught Guinness.

Opening times are Monday and Tuesday 2 pm to 4.30 pm and 7 pm to 11 pm; Wednesday, Thursday, Friday, Saturday and Sunday noon to 4.30 pm and 6 pm (7 pm Sunday) to 11 pm (10.30 pm Sunday).

Telephone: 01422 244863.

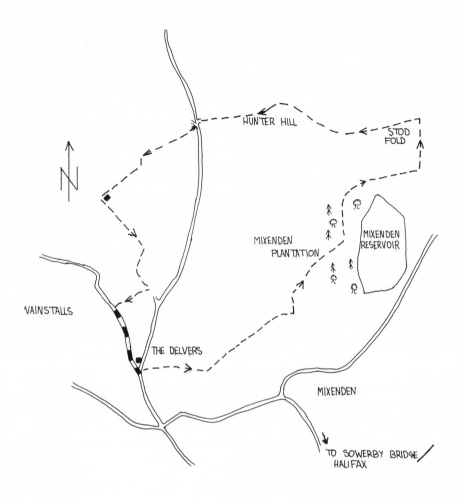

How to get there: The inn is in the village of Wainstalls north-west of Halifax.

Parking: Park in the inn car park.

Length of the walk: 4 miles. OS Map Landranger series 104 (inn GR 048283).

An introduction to the Calderdale Way — moors and mills — with some interesting period architecture along the way.

The Walk

Take the signposted footpath opposite the inn to the left and walk on wallside along the boundaries of three fields. Turn left through a gate and go right, keeping to the edges of two further fields. At the next field, veer diagonally left to an old building and, crossing a stile, turn right to the edge of a housing estate in Mixenden. Turn left along Hambleton Drive, continuing for about 400 yards. Turn left again down the next street, heading for an open common. Go through a gap in a wall and fork right in the direction of Mixenden Plantation. Enter the woods and go left on the public footpath, swinging right to a lane. Go down the lane past several cottages and turn left at the Stodfold Kennels access. Walk on to the farm buildings and swing right over the extensive concreted hardstanding to find a gate. Go left, following the yellow arrowhead and walk on at the back of the farm and kennels uphill over several stiles.

The conical form of Hunter Hill dominates the forward view. Swing right around the base of the hill and go left with the quarry to your left. Walk on to the road. Cross, turn left for 15 yards and go right into the access of Nolstar Boarding Kennels. Walk on for 10 yards and, following the 'Calderdale Way' sign, mount a stile, arcing sharp left to find a second stile in the corner. Continue forward following the distinctive yellow markers over several fields and stiles and turn left on a track, walking on towards a group of cottages. Go sharp right (you will notice embankments on your right – a dam) to discover a characterful inn, the Moorcock, and turn left over the car park to the road, passing the depot of Collett Heavy Haulage. Walk on round the bend continuing uphill. Turn right along the access to Slack Farm (unmarked but public right of access was confirmed to me) and go left over a stile, turning right to the side of the mill. Drop down to the road and turn left through Wainstalls back to the inn.

Other local attractions: Luddenden to the south (a conservation area village).

Calder Grove
The Navigation

A dry dock for bargees since 1838, the canalside Navigation is marooned on the outskirts of Wakefield. In appealing isolation only seconds from the M1, the inn retains her watery charms, chaperoned by restricted access and a whale-backed bridge. With 72-hour moorings, toilet and shower facilities, a range of economically priced bar snacks and fine fettled ale, the inn is an essential port of call for narrow boats. The attractive bars, sparkling with copper topped tables and hung with nostalgic photographs of steam driven craft, also attract landlubbers. The inn with its children's room and its large front garden, equipped with swings and slides, is popular with families.

Supplemented by daily specials, the standard menu includes hot sandwiches, scampi, haddock, and plaice, bacon and mushroom flan, sirloin steak and various burgers. Children have their own menu. The hand-pulled ale is clerical collared Tetley Bitter and Timothy Taylor's Landlord and a guest beer. Castlemaine and Skol lagers and Woodpecker and Strongbow ciders are the alternative brews.

The inn is open from Monday to Saturday from 11 am to 11 pm. Sunday hours are from 12 noon to 3 pm and 7 pm to 10.30 pm.

Telephone: 01924 274361.

How to get there: The inn is on Broad Cut Road, alongside the Calder and Hebble Navigation at Calder Grove, south-west of Wakefield near to junction 39 of the M1.

Parking: Park in the inn car park.

Length of the walk: 6 miles. OS Map Landranger series 110 (inn GR 304173).

A fairly strenuous hike by canal, field and glade to the wooded beauty spot of Coxley Valley.

The Walk

Turn right from the inn following the towpath for about 1 mile to a canal overbridge. Turn left, crossing the bridge and walk uphill on Balk Lane past a cricket ground to Netherton village. Cross the road, and, near the High Ridge street nameplate sign, take the marked footpath, turning right between houses and then over a makeshift stile (old bread trays are very versatile) to a farmyard. Go right fieldside and at the top end of the soccer pitch, turn right to the road. Turn right for a short distance and almost opposite the Working Men's Club, turn left following a signposted footpath downhill into Coxley. Walk on at

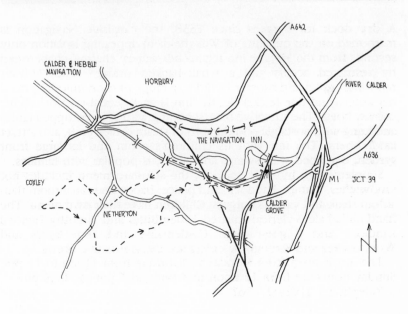

the bottom for about 30 yards, and turn left along an unsignposted track immediately before Oak Cottage. Continue uphill and enter delightful bluebell woods. Continue to a farm, and turn left over a stile, dropping downhill to a small lake, the preserve of pampered (no fishing, no shooting) fowl and fish.

Cross the feeder stream on a planked footbridge and veer left, following a well defined track to the crest. Walk on, back into Netherton. Cross Coxley Crescent and continue on a footpath to the road and the Star Inn. Turn right down South Road for 350 yards and follow the signposted track left through the lorry compound. On a winding route, pass three cottages, go through a farmyard and where the tarmac road begins, watch out for a footpath on your left hand (sign missing) by an overgrown pond. Turn left fieldside, curving round to a stile on the left. Go left across the meadow to the road. Cross and take the marked footpath into woodland dropping down to the canal side. Continue to the bridge opposite the Navigation inn. Cross, returning to your starting point.

Other local attractions: Yorkshire Sculpture Park (3 miles south – free entry).

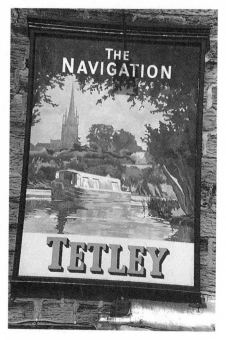

Bramhope
The Fox and Hounds

A yeoman's house of 1728 distinguished by open fires and a wealth of antiques, the Fox and Hounds is a fashionable den renowned for good ale and convivial company.

Bar meals, served lunchtimes only (children welcome), include ham and roast beef sandwiches (home-cooked joints), Yorkshire puddings, steak and kidney pie, sirloin steak, tagliatelle napolitaine and salade nicoise. Hand-pulled Tetley Bitter and Mild provide the main liquid refreshment. Lowenbrau, Castlemaine and Carlsberg lagers, Gaymer's Olde English cider and Guinness are also on tap. The inn has a stone flagged taproom (just made for walking boots) and a pleasant outside seating area to the rear.

Opening times are from Monday to Saturday 11.30 am to 11 pm. Sunday hours are 12 noon to 3 pm and 7 pm to 10.30 pm.

Telephone: 0113 284 2448.

How to get there: The inn is in the centre of Bramhope (The Cross) an attractive, well heeled village off the A660 north of Leeds.

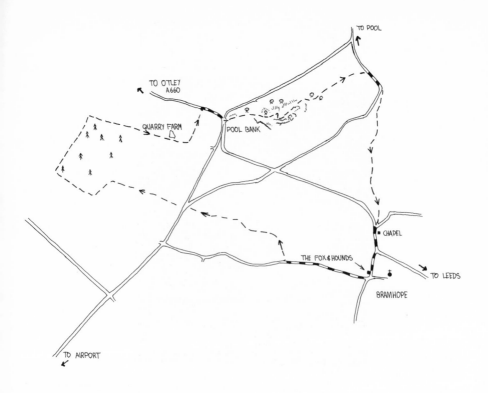

Parking: Park in the inn car park.

Length of the walk: 4 miles. OS Map Landranger series 104 (inn GR 248434).

An exhilarating up and downer over moorland paths and woodland tracks, offering superb views of the Wharfe valley.

The Walk

Turn right from the inn, and turn right again along Old Lane, passing the cricket ground. Walk on beyond the last house and turn right, following the waymarked footpath signposted to 'Pool Bank'. Cross a stile, and go left over a second stile, keeping left by a broken wall. Take the right hand fork across a field to the corner and go left to the side of a soccer pitch. Continue to the road – Old Pool Bank.

Cross the road and go left for 20 yards only. Turn right, following the marked footpath to a stile and cross, walking on towards

woodland over a second stile. Take the left hand fork in the wood, swinging left and right, and continue to meet a broad sandy track. Turn right downhill – the panorama of Wharfedale gradually unfolds. Swing left and go right at the crest, following the footpath past Quarry Farm. Go second left, past the houses, dropping down towards the road. Turn right along the footpath to the road.

Cross the road, and go left on the sharp bend just beyond the Bar House following the marked footpath. Walk on to Far Row Cottages, turn right and go left by the last cottage into woodland. Keep left, dropping down to a stile and a meadow. Cross the stile, walk along the grassy ridge to the next stile and enter the poetically named Avenue des Hirondelles. At the road, cross, go right and then left by Firs Hill Court up Stairfoot Lane (steep climb). At the summit, turn left and right, back to the inn.

Other local attractions: Puritan chapel founded in 1649 – near the inn on the A660 (open on Saturdays and Sundays only). Leeds and Bradford Airport passenger lounge (free air show).

Hainworth
The Guide Inn

Surveying most of Yorkshire, at an elevation of 922 ft, the Guide Inn is as cosy as grandma's knee. The bucolic appeal of two taproom murals ('Here's Ta Me An Ma Wife's Usban Not Fo'getting Mesen') and a draped White Ensign celebrating the naval background of the landlord, set the friendly scene, made even more appealing in winter when hot crumpets are available for DIY toasting over open fires. Another attractive feature of the Guide is the children's play area, presided over by a pet turkey. Recently introduced, go-carting has proved an instant success.

As with the pub, so with the menu: food has a personality at the Guide. Try the omelettes made with free range eggs, the pie and peas ('probably the best in the world') the home-made meat and potato pie or the farmhouse grill. Children's portions are available. On tap are hand pulled Tetley's and Bass Bitter, Tennent's and Carlsberg lagers, Strongbow cider and Guinness, and tea and coffee are also served.

The inn is open from Monday to Saturday from 11 am to 11 pm. Sunday hours are from 12 noon to 3 pm and 7 pm to 10.30 pm.

Telephone: 01535 272138.

How to get there: The inn is on the Keighley Road at a crossroads equidistant from Cullingworth, Haworth, Keighley and Harden.

Parking: Park in the inn car park.

Length of the walk: 4½ miles. OS Map Landranger series 104 (inn GR 066387).

A scenic traverse of moor, woodland and vale, rewarding the strenuous sections with impressive views.

The Walk

Take the marked public bridleway opposite the inn and walk on towards distant pylons. At the intersection, take the rough track to your right (not the one onto the moor), going right and swinging left under the power lines. Drop down wallside into the top end of the valley and swing right to the far crest, steering between the trees and the heather. Arc right on a descending track towards Harden. On reaching an access track in the bottom, go right, pass a large detached house to your right and swing sharp left on a bend over a beck in Deep Cliff Hole.

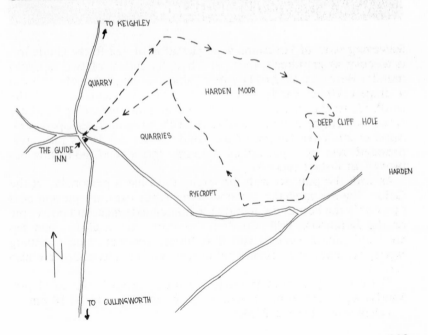

Walk on for 100 yards to the next bend and look out for a scrawled and easily missed sign to the left by a gate. Go through a gap in the wall and aim right for the farmyard. Walk on past the farm buildings and at the next gate, go through, going diagonally right over two fields to the corner. Mount a stile and take the footpath in front following the instructions 'Follow This Wall'. Climb uphill by the field edges, veering right to the top. Cross a stile and turn right, passing Ivy House and Ryecroft Farm. Go left through a cottage gate into woodland, climbing gradually onto the moor. Drop down right and aim left on a 45° tangent away from the power lines. At the outcrop of rocks opposite a farmhouse, swing left across the open moorland on a well worn track, steering towards distant mounds. Swing right to the track and left back to the inn.

Other local attractions: St. Ives estate to the east (golf course and further walks).

Barwick in Elmet
The Black Swan

In the shadow of England's tallest maypole, the Black Swan is a friendly village inn, well patronised by locals and visitors alike. Formerly three 18th century cottages converted around 1900, the low beamed inn offers three cosy inter-connecting rooms, handsomely furnished in blue velvet. The walls are hung with pictures by local artists.

Standard fare, served every lunchtime and on Wednesday, Thursday and Friday evenings, includes giant Yorkshire puddings, grills, roast chicken, pork and beef with fresh vegetables, lasagne, omelettes and fried fish. The daily blackboard menu features a range of home-made steak and kidney, chicken and ham and turkey and vegetable pies, savoury crumbles and fish dishes such as plaice stuffed with prawns and garlic. Duck and wildfowl are occasionally served in season. The line-up of sweets is headed by a choice of fruit tarts. Children are welcome for meals. The selection of liquid refreshments is wide, the well stocked bar serving John Smith's Bitter, Foster's, Miller Lite, Kronenbourg and Carlton LA lagers, Strongbow and Woodpecker cider and draught Guinness.

The Black Swan is open Monday to Saturday from 11 am to 11 pm. Sunday opening is from 12 noon to 3 pm, and 7 pm to 10.30 pm.

Telephone: 0113 281 3065.

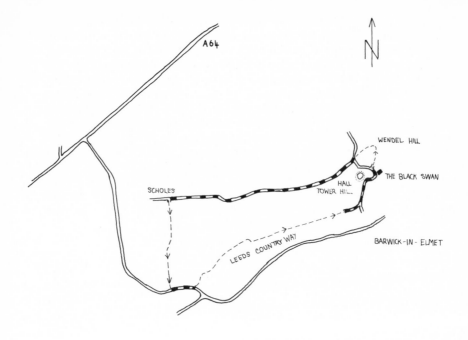

How to get there: The Black Swan is in the village of Barwick in Elmet on the eastern boundary of Leeds.

Parking: Park in the inn car park to the rear.

Length of the walk: 2½ miles. OS Map Landranger series 104/105 (inn GR 400375).

A leisurely pastoral ramble discovering ancient earthworks of the Normans, and a once royal citadel – the capital of the mighty kingdom of Elmet.

The Walk

Leaving by the rear entrance, follow the footpath sign marked 'Potterton Lane'. Skirting a deep defensive entrenchment, walk on to Meadow View and turn left towards Pear Tree Farm. Bear right to two stiles, crossing onto the crest of Wendel Hill. Descend on a diagonal path to a stile near the Rake Beck. (In days of old, a series of sluices held back the waters of the beck to provide for inundation of this vulnerable flank of the castle in times of danger.)

112

Cross the stile and turn left uphill past Burnside Farm. Turn right along Rake Hill Road and continue to a hamlet of cottages (formerly a 19th century paupers' workhouse). Proceed uphill on an undulating, partly wooded track and approach the outskirts of Scholes. Turn left by the playing fields' changing pavilion on a signposted footpath over a number of fields and stiles to Scholes. Turn left along the main street. Immediately past the garage, take the clearly defined footpath marked 'Leeds Country Way' back into Barwick and Carrfield Road. Turn left along Elmwood Lane to the Methodist church. (To the left is the eminence of Hall Tower Hill which formed part of the motte of a Norman fortification.) Turn right to the inn.

Other local attractions: The maypole (triennial raising ceremony attracts large crowds), the village cross and All Saints' church.

Hade Edge
The Bay Horse

On the brink of the infernally named Hade Edge, this lofty wayfarers' inn has served the travelling public for over 200 years. With fine views and an open-fired lounge attractively decorated with watercolours by a local artist, the popular Bay Horse serves hand-pulled ale and honest, modestly priced food. Ham and egg breakfasts (from 9 am) can be arranged for pre-booked walking parties; later diners can select from a standard menu which lists Yorkshire pudding, sirloin steak, 16 oz T bones and chicken curry. The house specials are meat and potato pie (Wednesdays and Fridays) and roast Sunday lunches. Children are welcome for meals. The inn has a cosy back bar devoted to darts and pool, and a pleasant outside seating area. At Christmas time the Bay Horse is a rendezvous for the Penistone Foxhounds.

Surprisingly for a Yorkshire pub, the main liquid fare is Burtonwood Bitter (brewed in Chester). Burtonwood Mild, Tophat Strong Ale, Skol and Tuborg lagers, draught Guinness and Strongbow cider are the alternative choices.

Opening times are from Monday to Saturday 11 am to 11 pm. Sunday hours are 12 noon to 3 pm and 7 pm to 10.30 pm.

Telephone: 01484 683377.

114

How to get there: The inn is on the B6106, 2 miles south of Holmfirth.

Parking: Park in the inn car park or on the rough triangular area opposite the inn.

Length of the walk: 4 miles. OS Map Landranger series 110 (inn GR 146059).

A journey to hell and back! No, really this is a very pleasant walk, taking in Hade Edge, which gets its name from the tumbledown farmhouse known as Hades, which you will also encounter. The woodland scents help to make this one enjoyable even on a rainy day.

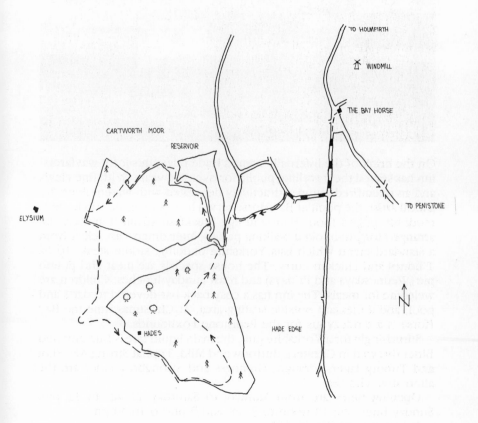

The Walk

Leave the inn, crossing the triangular area of land opposite, and turn left along Dunford Road towards the settlement of Hade Edge. Turn right down Greave Road, passing Hade Edge school to your right. Continue round the bend and take the marked footpath to your left, crossing a ladder stile on the 'Kirklees Way'. Drop down to the left, following a wall to a stile. Go right, and cut off the corner by turning sharp left to the edge of the reservoir. Continue left, swinging right to a gate. Go through the wall crossing, following the well defined path above the shoreline to the right.

Just before you reach a point opposite the dam wall and spillway, go left uphill on a woodland pathway. Veer off to the right by an upright stone pillar, dropping down to an ancient pack horse bridge. Cross, ascend right for 30 yards only and swing left, following a wall, eventually emerging to the edge of the plantation opposite the gable end of a farmstead known as Elysium. I don't want to worry you, but the conifered recesses you have just left (the plantation is spookily called Old Betty Nick) have witnessed the proceedings of a witches' coven. Sacrifices have been discovered dangling from trees thereabouts and strange arrangements of stones have been discovered . . . come with a friend.

Turn left by a wall and walk on to a green gate and turn left again. Turn right, heading away from the trees, and swing right downhill to a second pack horse bridge. Swing left uphill to the brooding ruins of Hades. An inspection of the massive stones stirs the imagination. Drop down, passing a restored barn to your left and, ignoring the trackway to the left into the plantation, keep straight on to find the next trackway, again to the left. Turn left between broad stands of conifers, arcing left 180°. Walk on to a pathway and turn right, back to the reservoir. Retrace your route back to the inn.

Other local attractions: Holmfirth – TV location for the series 'Last of the Summer Wine' and home to Bamforth's Postcard Museum.

Ogden
The Causeway Foot Inn

A purveyor of fun for all ages, this roadside mecca attracts customers from all points of the Calderdale compass. Offering hand-pulled ales, bar and restaurant meals, a large and extensively equipped garden and children's play area, and live entertainment which includes a Yorkshire version of Blind Date, the Causeway Foot is not for greybeards. Like the attractions, the decorations and fittings are electric – oak and plush velvet, amplifiers, a pool table and a variety of pictures, pride of place being reserved for a splendid watercolour of a lioness in pursuit of a meal.

Meals at the inn can also be taken al fresco, selecting from a standard bar menu which lists cottage pie, Lancashire hot pot, lasagne, giant Yorkshire puddings and various pizzas. Diners in the 30 cover restaurant can choose from grilled salmon, pork chasseur, lamb chops or roast of the day. Sunday lunches are also available and children are welcome. Top of the alcoholic bill at the Causeway Foot is hand-pulled John Smith's and Ruddles bitters, supported by Fosters and Kronenbourg lagers, Bulmer's cider and draught Guinness.

The inn is open from Monday to Saturday 12 noon to 2 am (special licence, but doors close 11 pm). Sunday hours are from 12 noon to 3 pm and 7 pm to 10.30 pm.

Telephone: 01422 240052.

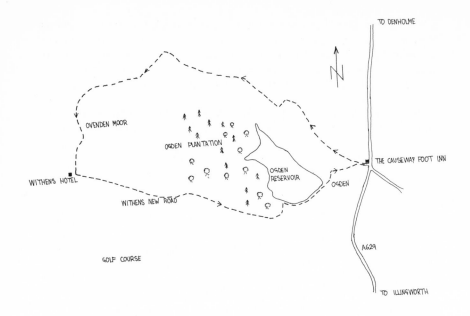

How to get there: The inn fronts the A629 in the hamlet of Ogden west of Bradford.

Parking: Park in the inn car park to the rear.

Length of the walk: 5½ miles. OS Map Landranger series 104 (inn GR 069309).

A wind blown circuit of Ovenden Moor – peat-hags, peewits and wild panoramas.

The Walk

Leaving the inn by the rear exit, turn left and turn right along Ogden Lane. Fork right after 100 yards, following a signposted public bridleway onto moorland. At the next gate, turn left, dropping down towards Ogden Reservoir. Turn right on a track, swinging right uphill and going left towards the neck of the valley. After about a mile, drop down to your left, crossing Ogden Clough on a footbridge. Ascend, walking away from the valley onto moorland. Follow the line of cairns, first arcing right and then left. The looming gable end of a pub on the horizon is no mirage!

Swing right to a second footbridge and go uphill towards the pub and a kissing gate. Turn left along the broad track known as Withens New Road, passing a golf course. After about 1½ miles, turn left over a stile into the Odgen Plantation. Go right to the edge of the reservoir and follow the footpath round through a gate to the dam wall. Cross the wall, walk uphill and turn right back to the inn.

Other local attractions: Keighley and Worth Valley Steam Railway in Oxenhope to the north.

Calverley
The Thornhill Arms

A prominent and convenient halt on the busy A657, the former Leopard Inn has had a long and well documented history since landlord John Cuttell drew his first pint in 1673. A natural retreat for congregations from the nearby church of St. Wilfred, the inn has always enjoyed a reputation for the less spiritual blessings of life, as a 1725 bill for a funeral wake shows:

> Back loin and hindlift of beef 7/6d; hinder quarter of good large veal 4/6d; two large legs of mutton 5/-; shoulder of veal 2/-; shoulder and neck of mutton 2/6d; loin of mutton roasted 1/6d; fine large ham 7/-; six boiled pullets 3/-; two geese bought dressed 2/8d; two more geese at home 2/6d; half a dozen ducks 4/-; three couples of rabbits 2/3d; six pullets roasted 4/-; two dishes of fish (cod and lyng) 2/-; capers, cucumbers and pickles 5/-; apples and gooseberries for sweet tarts 2/-; 15 pounds of butter 6/3d; and drink for 60 persons apiece one with another 20/-.

Today, in a much altered and cavernous bar adorned with warming pans, brasses and a pair of flintlock guns, the accent is still on girding the loins, and diners may choose from a substantial daily menu which typically includes steak and kidney pie, roast beef and Yorkshire pudding, pie and peas, moussaka, lasagne and spotted dick. Children are welcome for meals.

The bar top attractions are hand-pulled Theakston's, John Smith's and Courage Directors Bitter, Carlsberg and Foster's lagers, draught Guinness and Strongbow and Woodpecker ciders.

The inn is open from Monday to Saturday 11.30 am to 3 pm and 6 pm to 11 pm. Sunday hours are 12 noon to 3 pm and 7 pm to 10.30 pm.

Telephone: 0113 256 5492.

How to get there: The inn is roadside on the A657 in the village of Calverley to the west of Leeds.

Parking: Park in the inn car park.

Length of the walk: 2½ miles. OS Map Landranger series 104 (inn GR 209368).

A sylvan saunter to the canal . . . and a more energetic hike back.

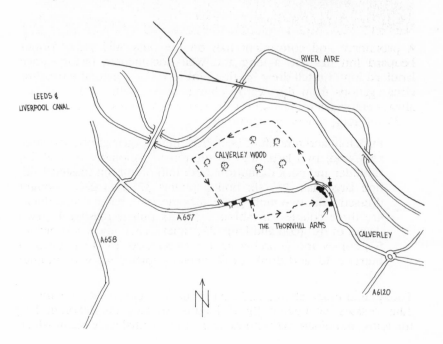

The Walk

Cross the busy road opposite the inn, and go left. Pass the church and go right along the unmarked footpath to the school. Continue along the track and go through a wicket gate, proceeding by the edge of a copse to a gate by a house. Go through and swing left following the edge of a wood and swinging left again to find a stile just before the corner. Go left over the stile, take the right hand fork and the next right hand fork, dropping down left and right through bracken to the bottom edge of the wood. Turn left and walk on to merge with a bridle track. Continue to a gate and a stile. Cross, and pass Dene Hurst and other houses on Thornhill Drive. (At the beginning of this access road, it is interesting to turn right to view the messings about on the nearby canal.)

From Thornhill Drive, turn sharp left up a steep hill (high wall to your right). Proceed through a sort of mini canyon under a bridge to the road. Go left, cross, and after 200 yards, turn right down Salisbury Street. Turn left through the cricket ground and at the far exit turn left and first right down West End Road. Turn left opposite the Mechanics Institute and turn right along Blackett Street. This will deliver you to the rear of the inn. Go left through a back gate to the car park.

Other local attractions: Abbey House Museum, Kirkstall (period street), Kirkstall Abbey (Cistercian) and Armley Mills Industrial Museum (once the world's largest wool mill: history of Leeds clothing, textile, engineering and optics manufacturing – working steam trains).

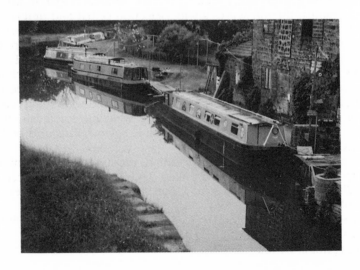

Barkisland
The New Rock

Known as the 'Hard End' – an allusion to the fate of condemned prisoners who were granted a last gargle before being executed – this solid redoubt of licensedom stands in the shadow of Gallows Pole Hill. A 17th century converted farmhouse decorated with motor rally memorabilia, the inn serves a wide selection of bar and dining room meals. The standard menu features gambas, curried melon and prawns, home-made soup, steak and kidney pie, chicken tikka massala, a range of steaks, mushroom stroganoff and deep fried potato skins with garlic mayonnaise and crispy salad. The daily blackboard specials typically offer cheese and broccoli bake, grilled salmon and meat and potato pie followed by spotted dick and something referred to as pampered possy pie. Children are welcome for meals. If you want a longer stay, facilities are available for caravans and bed and breakfast can be arranged.

Renowned for its throat embrocation, the inn dispenses a number of tantalising brews – hand-pulled Tetley, Marston Pedigree and Theakston bitters, Lowenbrau, Labatt's and Castlemaine lagers and Murphy's and Beamish stouts.

Opening times are Monday to Saturday 5 pm to 11 pm. Sunday hours 11 am to 11 pm.

Telephone: 01422 823578.

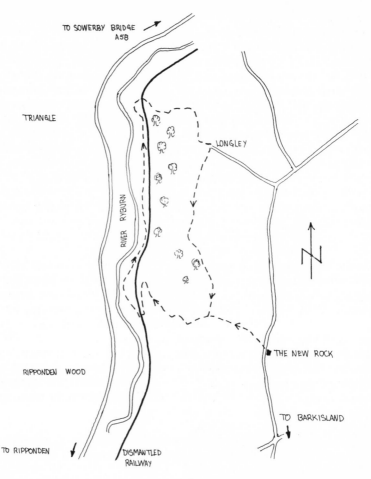

How to get there: On a minor road, the inn is south of Sowerby Bridge, in an elevated position above the village of Barkisland (A6025).

Parking: Park in the inn car park.

Length of the walk: 4 miles. OS Map Landranger series 104 (inn GR 053208).

Here is a landscape to compare with anything the dales can offer and, amazingly, you can enjoy it in blessed solitude, even on sunny Bank Holidays. This walk demands fitness — steep ascents!

124

The Walk

Take the waymarked footpath – 'Calderdale Way' opposite the inn, dropping down on a track signposted to Highlee. Swing right into woodland and follow the path until it turns sharp left at the side of a house. Go through the gate and keep left, descending on the access track to the bottom. Turn right over the redundant railway bridge and go right again alongside the river Ryburn. At the bridge, swing right, away from the bank uphill into woodland. At the next railway bridge, drop down and continue forward, following the course of the old track under a viaduct. Merge with a path to the left opposite renovated buildings, continuing to a gate and stile. Go over and, opposite the cricket pitch, turn sharp right over another railway bridge.

At this point, three routes will beckon. Just stop for a moment to examine the ancient cobbles. What a splendid industrial heritage feature they are, and how practical even still for horses. And now you have learnt about cobbles, to take a leaf out of Mr Wackford Squeers' book . . . climb them! – the middle route please.

At the top, turn right, in the direction of a farmhouse and go left into the hamlet of Longley. Pass Longley Cottage and turn immediately right up several steps into a field. Follow a wall, crossing a meadow to a stile. Cross into a copse, keeping to the edge and weaving left to a gap in the wall. Go through and keeping wallside, walk up to a gate. Veer right, keeping to the topside of the wood to another gate. STOP! It is easy to get lost at this point. The route is just a few inches to your right, but the stile crossing is obscured by a holly tree. Go right first dropping down and then ascending by a barbed wire fence to the left. Using wall crossings, go over two fields and turn left on the track back to the inn.

Other local attractions: Piece Hall, Halifax (built in 1779 as a grandiose cloth mart; now extensively restored and converted for modern shopping).

Carlton
The Queen

Street corner sovereign of a village famous for rhubarb, the by-passed Queen traded her crown for a bar-maid's cap at the end of the coaching era. Snug and disarmingly friendly, today she is the archetypal local, a centre of the social scene, recently re-liveried in pastels and stained glass.

The games room and the adjacent lounge with its 'royal corner' gallery of photographs and its tribute to Carlton's celebrated 'Ale Voice Choir' offer a range of simple bar meals. Like the rhubarb, the fare is earthy and nutritious – special recipe stews, pies and pasties vying for popularity alongside Yorkshire pudding and generously filled sandwiches. Children are welcome for meals. The lubricants for the illustrious songsters are hand-pulled Tetley Bitter, Castlemaine and Skol lagers, Gaymer's Olde English and Copperhead ciders and draught Guinness.

The inn is open from Monday to Saturday 12 noon to 3 pm (5 pm on Saturday) and 7 pm to 11 pm. Sunday hours are 12 noon to 3 pm and 7 pm to 10.30 pm.

Telephone: 0113 282 1063.

How to get there: The inn is in the village of Carlton near Rothwell, south of Leeds.

Parking: Park in the small car park behind the inn or on street.

Length of the walk: 3½ miles. OS Map Landranger series 104 (inn GR 337271).

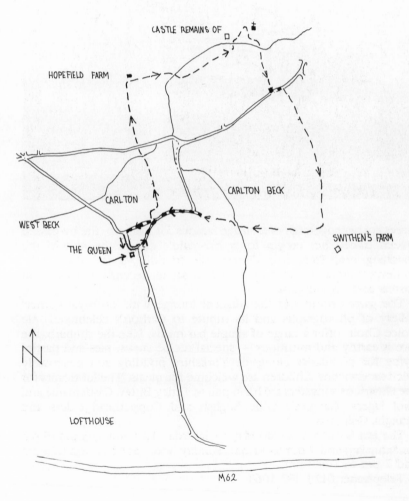

An interesting city fringe ramble visiting rhubarb fields, the ruins of an ancient castle and a variety of ecclesiastical, domestic and commercial architecture which add to the appeal.

The Walk

Turn right from the inn to New Road and turn left past Carlton school. On the bend opposite the Chapel Street sign take the footpath beside the garden area. Swing right and left fieldside, and cross West Beck to the road. Cross and continue on a track to Hopefield Farm. Turn right and drop down right to a footbridge. Cross and go left beckside to the next footbridge. Cross and turn right to the site of Rothwell Castle. Swing left and right to the road and turn right past the front of Holy Trinity church – see the splendid Jacobean font and fascinating sculptures and monuments. Turn right along Butcher Lane past the Hare and Hounds inn and turn left on Marsh Street. Turn right at the British Oak down Swithins Lane and continue, leaving the built up area onto a farm track. At the crest, turn right and follow a marked footpath downhill. At the bottom, go right over a stile and veer left, mounting a white gate, and immediately crossing the Carlton Beck to a track. Turn right and swing left to Carlton's Main Street. Walk on and proceed down Chapel Street. Turn left back to the inn.

Other local attractions: Newly established golf driving range and golf course at Oulton and Temple Newsam House and Park 3 miles to the north-east (mansion, rare breeds centre and gardens – an admission fee is payable for the house only).

Publisher's Note

We hope that you obtain considerable enjoyment from this book; great care has been taken in its preparation. However, changes of landlord and actual closures are sadly not uncommon. Likewise, although at the time of publication all routes followed public rights of way or permitted paths, diversion orders can be made and permissions withdrawn.

We cannot of course be held responsible for such diversion orders and any resultant inaccuracies in the text which result from these or any other changes to the routes nor any damage which might result from walkers trespassing on private property. We are anxious that all details covering the walks and the pubs are kept up to date and would therefore welcome information from readers which would be relevant to future editions.